Garden Accessories

Garden Accessories

Designing with Collectibles, Planters, Fountains & More

Teri Dunn

FRIEDMAN/FAIRFAX
PUBLISHERS

MetroBooks

An Imprint of Friedman/Fairfax Publishers

Library of Congress Cataloging-in-Publication Data available upon request.

ISBN 1-58663-030-X

Editors: Susan Lauzau and Hallie Einhorn
Photography Editor: Erin Feller
Production Manager: Maria Gonzalez

Color separations by Fine Arts Repro
Printed in China by Leefung-Asco Printing Ltd.

1 3 5 7 9 10 8 6 4 2

For bulk purchases and special sales, please contact:
Friedman/Fairfax Publishers
Attention: Sales Department
15 West 26th Street
New York, NY 10010
212/685-6610 FAX 212/685-1307

Visit our website:
www.metrobooks.com

Contents

INTRODUCTION

If selecting and growing plants is the heart of gardening, adding accessories or decorations is the soul. The items you include—whether sculpture, fountain, pot, birdbath, or even outdoor furniture—say volumes about the mood you're trying to create. The right object in the right spot can make a garden appear refreshingly fun, confer an elegant stamp of formality, or supply a comforting aura of serenity.

Carefully chosen objects also add a sense of permanence to the scene. Flowers bloom and fade around your garden accents, vines and groundcovers encroach upon them in good years and retreat in times of drought or stress, shrubs and trees grow up around them. But the object steadfastly abides, whether it is a beautiful old urn, a jaunty gazing ball, a brightly painted birdhouse, or a cast-iron seat, gate, or arch. You can use garden accessories in so many ways, including to define boundaries, to add interest or color to dim corners, to bring continuity to an ever-changing palette of plants, and to bridge the look and feel of different seasons.

And garden accents can also be downright practical. Should you want to disguise features you'd rather went unnoticed, you're in luck. An ornate trellis or billowing basket can hide the fact that your garden is small, or can draw attention away from something beyond its bounds (say, the neighbor's garage, trash bins, a chain-link fence) that isn't attractive. A bubbling fountain will distract from street noise, while an overflowing planter box anchored to the side of a porch or deck will keep the outside world out.

Garden accessories also have a wonderful way of elevating or injecting excitement into simple designs. A colorful addition, such as a blue chair or a red planter box or some brightly painted tiles, helps you create a stylish picture, even when your plant palette is limited. Pots, solo or grouped together, filled with a variety of flowers and foliage plants, lend an established look to cramped quarters or dull corners. Be adventurous with the sort of spray pattern your new fountain generates, and it will become a scene-stealer. Nestle an interesting sculpture into an otherwise undistinguished groundcover for a composition that suddenly now stands out, intrigues, and draws visitors. And so on.

Indeed, ornaments confer a sense of polish or finish to any planting or landscape, whether it is well established or brand new. Regard the addition of "unnatural" elements as cheating if you will, but the effect is undeniable. If you have the chance to visit other gardens, particularly those that are the work of experienced gardeners, you will always see objects of various kinds and styles employed. Whether a pretty pot or an attractive bench, the very presence of the item shows that the gardener considered the overall picture, and deliberately introduced the refining touch.

Ultimately, accessories enhance the gardens they decorate to the point where they become as much a part of that world as any living plant. Be creative, and have fun with them. They're essential to the spirit of the place.

ABOVE: Richly varied yet beautifully cohesive in design, this purple-themed hanging garden further softens a luminous lilac wall. The gently cascading flowers include geraniums (*Pelargonium* 'Lady Plymouth'), nemesia, lobelia, and 'Tinkerbell' brachycome.

OPPOSITE: A sundial set on a moss-grown pedestal gives focus and a pleasing sense of antiquity to a lush country garden studded with masterwort (*Astrantia* spp.) and two kinds of cranesbills (*Geranium pratense* and *G. macrorrhizum*).

In the following pages, a wide range of objects and styles are arrayed. Some things are easily bought from garden-supply stores, either locally or via mail-order. Others you might be lucky to find lurking at an antique or junk shop, a yard sale, or a grand estate sale. You'll see garden antiques and collectible objects, from statuary to vintage garden furniture. You'll browse through an assortment of creative hanging baskets and planters, some in surprising shapes or materials, some displayed, mounted, or filled in unexpected and appealing ways. There are also many different sorts of garden gates and arches, some wood, some metal, some formal, some casual—each calculated to mark a garden entrance and welcome visitors. Finally, peruse an enticing selection of large and small fountains and cascades, and you'll likely discover there's at least one that suits your garden, budget, and taste.

This is an ideas book, a tour of inspiring possibilities. Take time to examine what other gardeners have done—not only what they chose, but how they placed it and how it looks in the company of the plants they grow. Their visions will help you think about and clarify "the look" you'd like for your own garden. A firm handle on the color themes and general mood you are after will help you enormously when you go shopping.

But remember, too, to be open to new ideas and spontaneous purchases, for a certain sort of basket, gate, or water display may capture your imagination. And your garden accessory may end up telling you what kind of garden it wants to inhabit. Such decisions are a major part of the challenge, and the joy, of creating a beautiful garden.

ABOVE: Gates set the tone for the garden, marking the entrance deliberately and announcing the garden's prevailing style. This aqua and gold metal arch is at once stately and somewhat whimsical, promising a space that combines formal elements with fanciful ones.

OPPOSITE: A small grotto harbors the face of the god Apollo, who obligingly spews cool, clear water into a giant clam shell. The cascades continue over a series of volcanic rocks, flowing gently into a pool surrounded by feathery ferns and the leathery leaves of hostas.

Part One

GARDEN
ANTIQUES AND
COLLECTIBLES

INTRODUCTION

The appeal of antiques in a garden is obvious: embellishments of a certain age give the space an irresistible sense of having been comfortably in place for a long time. Vintage garden ornaments and collectibles are especially helpful in a young or freshly redone garden, where you may be impatient for your plants to mature and spread out or where you long for a sense of peaceful retreat. A time-worn statue, weathered urn, old-fashioned seat, or retired cart, carefully situated, grants the garden the air of permanence you seek—with style.

When a garden accent looks as if it has settled into its spot over time, count the idea a success. Moss or lichens embracing a statue and ivy twining around an old birdbath or armillary sphere bestow a mellowing effect. An air of stability and grace settles over the garden.

Trendy catalogs, garden accessory shops, and cluttered flea markets abound with chances for you to acquire authentic antiques or good reproductions, from highly formal or contrived pieces to ones that exude rustic or whimsical charm. But buyer beware: a high price tag doesn't guarantee authenticity.

Vintage ornaments are gaining in popularity, so if you hope to have a few, you'd do wise to start looking now. Pieces from European manors or the estates of the Old South can fetch thousands of dollars; others, like 1950s metal furniture, are currently quite trendy and sure to rise in price. If you do acquire something expensive, or are lucky enough to receive an heirloom or another item that has sentimental value, be sure to site it with care and secure it in place if you can. There's actually a small but growing subculture of garden bandits who know or suspect the value of that which they purloin.

In the end, the beauty of introducing "old" treasures to your garden is the fact that they do more than create an enchanting vignette or enhance the mood. They combine an enduring piece of man-made art with the ageless beauty of nature, enriching the garden for you as well as for admiring visitors.

ABOVE: Since the gate is the portal to the garden, and is often responsible for visitors' first impressions, you might invest in an old gate to give your garden that desirable feeling of being well-established. Check flea markets, estate sales, architectural salvage yards, and large rural junk shops for vintage examples. You may have to repair or replace hardware or latches, but the impact the gate brings to the garden will be well worth the trouble.

OPPOSITE: Nestled into an overgrown corner and joined by a putto—a figure of an infant boy, popular in Renaissance art—this retired porcelain bathtub gains new cachet as a garden ornament. The angled juxtaposition of the rustic bench in the foreground grants the pair a little privacy, lending the scene a sense of retreat from the busy world.

ABOVE: Herb plants, thanks to their naturally exuberant growth habits, look splendid in the company of rustic garden ornaments. Here, a retired garden cultivator fits the bill perfectly—its rusty metal and weatherbeaten wood are right at home in the garden's informal lushness.

OPPOSITE: Full sun, high summer, the heady fragrance of blooming lavender—it's the perfect setting for a sundial. If you can't find a sundial with a pedestal high enough or grand enough, shop for one separately or have a metal shop fashion a sturdy base for you. Just be sure the sundial plate itself is securely attached and, of course, level, should you intend to read it.

LEFT: Without inviting seats nearby, some of your favorite flower displays may be swiftly bypassed by garden visitors. This pair of august seats conveys permanence and a sense that the garden is well-established even when the surrounding plants are not particularly old or imposing—an impression desired by most gardeners. The benches promise the supreme respite, an opportunity to compose oneself in a quiet, semishady corner.

OPPOSITE: Lead or stone "baskets of fruit" are sometimes seen in historic European estates; their suggestion of a generous, bountiful harvest make them a natural for placement in the heart of the garden. This modern replica stands up to the elements and weighs less, which makes it a pleasing alternative to an authentic piece, especially if you find the original antiques cost-prohibitive or difficult to find. In either case, because these designs are inevitably a bit top-heavy, make certain to position the pieces securely on the ground.

ABOVE: An old, carved door and handmade storage jars and jugs in various sizes create a scene-stealing composition. The saturated blue paint, rubbed through to unfinished wood in places, is a pleasing counterpoint to the neutral, earthy shades of the vessels. This type of grouping is well worth re-creating, particularly if you haven't the time or inclination to fill every corner with plants yet you want great drama.

RIGHT: Fresh paint brings a sense of exuberance to otherwise staid old patio chairs, without sacrificing their original form. The rich cobalt blue used here doesn't shout out its presence, yet it provides welcome contrast to the frothy white and bold crimson blooms in the urn.

ABOVE: This beautiful old clay pot, liberally planted with bright blooms, gains additional character when a small carved statue is placed next to it. Though of different materials and construction (one formed by the potter's hand, the other by the carver's knife), the combination works because of their folksy character, and because neither piece is new. They are like two old friends that have weathered the years together, and have settled into the garden to stay.

OPPOSITE: Tuck an aged, empty oil jar into a corner of your perennial bed and enjoy the many facets it brings to the garden. The soft, warm umber color seems to go with any flower color, while the size and shape contribute ample contrast in form. Tipped on its side, the vessel appears long forgotten, perhaps discarded by some ancient civilization. Certainly, without this magnificent jar, the same spot would be far less intriguing.

LEFT: In the grand old British garden of Hampton Court, a fountain composed of an antique keystone and a weathered basin bring repose in the long shadows of late afternoon. Here both the style and age of the display confer a wonderful, ageless tranquility.

ABOVE: In an area where plantings are uncomplicated, dare to place a more elaborate seat, such as this venerable old beauty at Washington D.C.'s famed Dumbarton Oaks. The obvious age and classical lines of this piece give the setting real elegance.

ABOVE: Pieces made of copper and bronze, or alloys thereof, typically gain a handsome green patina as they age. Nor does this process take decades; in fact, several winters out in the garden in a cool or rainy climate ought to do the trick. Alternatively, some suppliers sell pieces that already have this timeworn look.

OPPOSITE: A touch of whimsy is always welcome, and it needn't be on ground level among the plants. Birds may or may not actually use these grand old quarters, but you can be sure that human garden visitors will be instantly drawn to the spot and will enjoy the sense of history it suggests with such unabashed charm.

GARDEN ORNAMENT

The best garden ornaments are those that simply strike your fancy. Deliberately or unwittingly, you are likely to choose something that "fits" with your taste in garden plants, making placement less challenging than you might originally suspect when you are shopping, out of sight of your yard. You may prefer graceful scenes with demure statues, or perhaps you like bolder, more dramatic statements made with a formal sundial or birdbath situated in the center of a flower bed. There is a vast range of styles from which you might choose, and certainly an appropriate antique or funky collectible can be found to suit every garden.

A word to the wise: as you shop, be wary of ornaments that display names or dates, as they may have been purloined from an estate or old cemetery. Rough edges that suggest a piece was chipped off a pedestal or wall are further cues that you may be looking at "hot" merchandise. For big-ticket items, insist on documentation of origin and composition, and get a receipt.

By its very nature, a garden is in a constant state of change, through the seasons and over the years. Well-chosen ornaments impart a sense of constancy in the midst of this constant flux, conferring a welcome feeling of age and stability. Leaves and flowers may burgeon all around a piece, or gradually insinuate themselves into its base and crevices, but the aged ornament will stand firm and serene as its world grows around it.

ABOVE: The pairing of a venerable ram's head sculpture (which probably originated in Mexico or South America) and small, jaunty daffodils is a stirring juxtaposition of antiquity and fresh, new life.

OPPOSITE: Elegantly formed statues of gods or goddesses are ideal for formal settings. Savvy placement will make a statue a garden focal point, granting weight and character to an otherwise undistinguished spot. Secure anchoring is critical, though, and shelter offered by nearby plants is wise, as such pieces can otherwise topple in stormy weather.

ABOVE: The graceful lines of the girl's body have been worn and smoothed by rain, wind, and sun, as has her offered seashell birdbath, yet the little birds still return year after year. A clearing in a quiet woodland garden is the perfect setting for the contemplative patience of this weatherbeaten figure.

OPPOSITE: In the legend, the inscrutable Sphinx (with the body of a lion, wings of a bird, and head of a woman) held its ground for many years while passersby tried and failed to answer its riddles. A modern replica ought to be placed along a path or wall, then, in a location where encroaching plants and the weather will eventually mute but never completely hide its mysterious demeanor.

ABOVE LEFT: Symbolic sculptures such as this Buddha figure are much more than mere decoration. They may be seen to soothe, bless, and protect their surroundings as well as those visitors who stop to ponder them. Plus, the older the piece, the more sincere or imposing the deity's presence seems.

ABOVE RIGHT: Mythological creatures such as this diminutive stone heraldic beast (note the coat of arms beneath its paws) are intriguing images in the garden. Situated in the midst of a fern bed and firmly anchored to a stone urn filled with water, this fellow looks like he is quietly guarding the scene.

OPPOSITE: The delicate beauty of pink azalea blossoms are a sure match for a Japanese-style stone lantern. Because this lantern's edges are worn and its surface is blanketed with velvety moss, a beguiling impression of antiquity reigns. A brand new ornament or one with a polished surface would miss completely the opportunity to foster this air of steadfastness and strength.

ABOVE: Shrubs are the foundation of almost every garden plan, and shrubby plants such as this ceanothus (or California lilac, as it is sometimes known) call for strong ornament that help anchor the scene. Heroic and mythological figures are naturally imposing and can stand up to the company of handsome, substantial plants. Where a statue won't fit, consider a large plaque, securely mounted on a support such as a wall or fence.

RIGHT: When you mount panels of ornamental tiles or a splendid architectural fragment over a garden fence or entrance, the eye is inevitably drawn upward. Flesh-and-blood people and whimsical terra-cotta characters both seem to pause and regard one another. Visitors to this garden will undoubtedly emerge with the pleasant sensation that they have been pilgrims traveling in a timeless world.

OPPOSITE: A stone arch requiring a gate is much better served by a panel of cast iron than by more vulnerable wood. The iron is a stronger, more imposing partner to the massive arch, and lends a prestigious air to the gateway. In addition, the scrolled iron bars permit a tempting peek into the garden, a treat not possible with a more solidly constructed door.

RIGHT: If you are the sort of gardener who allows plants and creatures in your garden—both the planned ones and the uninvited ones—to go their own way, you may be inclined to incorporate elaborate garden ornaments with interesting lines and features. Here, a decorative iron gate creates a vivid scene when a spider and the prickly red stem of a raspberry cane are given free rein.

ABOVE LEFT: Simplicity rules in this modest sundial display, whose elegant lines are all the more obvious in a garden's off-season. Note how the pedestal's sandy hue exudes a natural warmth that cast concrete never can.

ABOVE RIGHT: This armillary sphere, with its contrived arrow and supporting figure, is of supremely exuberant design. A piece like this is most at home in an informal setting, where its mood of motion will consort well with lively blossoms and foliage tossing in the breeze.

OPPOSITE: What kind of ornament can you place in the company of topiary or spiky perennials such as these foxgloves? It needs to be somewhat formal, and must answer to the timelessness of the shrubs as well as the fleeting beauty of the flowers—a sundial on a modest pedestal is the beautiful solution. In addition, the aged green patina of the dial's surface blends well with the color scheme of this stately garden.

ABOVE: Birdbaths come in a tremendous range of sizes, shapes, styles, and colors. Yours will fit in best if you take care to choose one that is not too large for its surroundings. Older pieces may be worn, chipped, or even cracked, so perform any patching or repair work before placing it in the garden and adding water.

OPPOSITE: The unassuming balustrade design of this birdbath pedestal hints that it was once part of a greater display along a grand porch or balcony. How aptly that feel works with a garden of young perennials still filling in their allotted areas—not to mention the single sculpted bird, just waiting to be joined by a host of feathered companions.

ABOVE LEFT: Foliage plants are rarely garden standouts on their own, but add a sculpture to the bed, and the area gains fresh interest. The angel's quiet gaze as well as its chalky, hard surface call attention to the contrasting glossy texture and lush growth that envelops it.

ABOVE RIGHT: A weeping cherry tree is the perfect spot to nestle in a little garden sculpture. The mood is a bit wistful; the cherry petals will fall, and the adjacent spring-flowering bulbs will fade, but the little boy's sweet illusion of agelessness will linger at the spot.

RIGHT: He never grows older, and the water never stops flowing—this small, "antiqued" fountain statue of a little boy at the pond's edge creates an eternal and charming presence. This is a modern replica of a well-loved design, so the fountain is guaranteed to be in good working order. If you invest in an antique fountain, you will probably need to have the plumbing updated to ensure a generous flow of water.

ANTIQUE AND VINTAGE FURNITURE

A seat in the garden is always inviting—a weathered bench or an intriguing antique chair has an irresistible, almost haunting appeal. Maybe that is because old chairs, benches, and accompanying tables hint at other visitors before you who have paused and rested.

Indeed, garden furnishings, above all other ornaments, beckon to guests, enticing them to view and savor the scene from a different angle. Garden seats provide them with an opportunity to see in a completely new way while relaxing, not standing and stopping, not strolling. Seats invite visitors to participate, to get down on the garden's level.

And as simple decor, garden furniture has the virtue of exuding an aura of leisure. It evokes slow afternoons that drift into quiet evenings of deepening shadows, of long, golden summers and snow-cushioned winters, of years and generations that come and go.

No wonder then, that choosing garden furniture is such a personal and visceral decision. Shop with an open mind and heart. Touch a seat, run your hand over its surfaces, picture it in a secluded corner of your garden or on your patio or deck. Sit down, breath deeply, and imagine yourself enfolded comfortably in its confines.

When you get the chair home, put it to use immediately. Later, you can brush off rust or dirt residue, install braces, add fresh paint and bright cushions, and decorate the environs with twining plants, nearby pots of herbs, and a tall glass of iced juice. Today, all you need to know is that an old friend has arrived.

OPPOSITE: An artifact of grand old parks and estates, the "tree seat" is designed in interlocking sections to fit around the trunk of a large shade tree. If you are lucky enough to find a full set, the charming old seat will immediately confer a feeling of stateliness to the largest tree on your lawn (even if the tree still has more growing to do).

RIGHT: Conversation, confidences, old stories—this informal set of vintage chairs and small table promises moments or hours of comfortable companionship. A metal plant stand painted to match offers a charming and appropriate accompaniment to the set, and provides an ideal resting place for plants, unused pots, and any other ornaments the gardener might fancy.

LEFT: The play of light and shadow is never more soothing than when it is dancing on the surface of something old and treasured. Carved wooden benches are indeed cherished pieces; if you cannot find one that is intact or in sufficiently good condition for use, you may be able, with care, to graft a decorative back onto a newer seat.

OPPOSITE: The artistic lines and intricate detailing on a weathered stone bench invite you to pause and marvel at its obvious age. The encroaching pink phlox link the bench to the garden successfully, but cannot steal the show from the grand old seat.

ABOVE: Embraced by abundant wildflowers, this nearly hidden cast-iron bench beckons silently, promising a spot for quiet repose. A secluded corner is an ideal setting for a vintage bench—allowing the garden to grow up around it only enhances the feeling of privacy. Indulge enthusiastic growers somewhat, but note that you'll almost certainly need to trim back overhanging plants after a time.

OPPOSITE: Matching garden furniture to adjacent plants is an art that requires a good eye and a healthy dose of creativity—this juxtaposition of an antique cast-iron English bench with the classically handsome spires of acanthus is a resounding success. The plant's broad, oversized leaves balance the intense verticality of the flower stalks, and both provide an interesting counterpoint in texture and form to the Gothic-inspired bench.

ABOVE LEFT: Refresh an old patio chair with coat of paint every now and then (be sure to use a paint specially formulated for exterior use). Not only does the piece last longer, you get a new chance to create appealing color combinations in the yard.

ABOVE RIGHT: Elaborate and well-crafted caning is a fading art, so if you find such a chair, grab it, bring it home, and see what can be done to repair it if need be. Because it is vulnerable to wet weather, place the caned chair under shelter (which will also give the sitter appreciated shade) and bring it indoors when necessary. Such chairs are lovely garden accents because they are made of natural materials and have a gentle, weathered color that blends well with flowers and foliage, particularly in informal or cottage-style gardens.

OPPOSITE: A hanging seat is an unorthodox choice, and plain wicker is an unconventional material for outdoor exposure, yet this seat, reminiscent of a sheltering cocoon or a protective eggshell, offers a haven that is virtually irresistible. Set in a peaceful woodland garden, off the path and beside a rushing stream, this rather eccentric hanging chair is sure to be a favorite of those garden visitors looking for a break from the busy world.

ABOVE: Off-season's hush invites flights of fancy—an old-fashioned iron bench and chairs conjure images of a lazy summer day, perhaps with finely dressed Victorian ladies and gentlemen perched on the seats.

RIGHT: This lonely, snow-covered bench waits under an arbor for spring to return. A more modern or trendy seat would lack the venerable heft and patient demeanor of this classic old one. In spring and summer, the climbers that swathe the arbor create a shady, secluded retreat.

ABOVE: They don't build them like they used to: this stylish variation on the classic Adirondack chair is the definition of outdoor-seating comfort. A slightly tilted back and deep, contoured seat urge you to stay, and wide arms can support a cool drink, a paperback book, and your languid arms. Cedar or redwood chairs last for many years.

LEFT: Ah, the alluring "courting swing." In keeping with its old-fashioned function, you'd do wise to invest in a vintage one. If an old one isn't available, give a newer one a fetching antiqued look with a coat of soft-hued paint.

ABOVE: Placed in the midst of thick-growing Matilija poppy foliage and overhung by abundant white lilies, this sweetheart cafe chair imparts a touch of whimsy to the corner of this city garden. Note the way the color of the chair brings out the blue tones in the potted agave nearby. Take a cue from this setting, and choose the colors of garden ornaments and plants to complement or accent one another.

WHIMSICAL TOUCHES

Adding ornament to a garden should be fun—the process itself should be as engaging as the final result. Perhaps you know exactly what you want—a ship's lantern or an old wheelbarrow that you will fill with annuals—and you are fortunate enough to find it. But go hunting with an open mind anyway. You will be pleasantly surprised at the nifty things you find and at the offbeat uses to which you can put familiar objects.

Maybe you have a particular spot in mind for the antique tool, funky birdhouse, or little statue you are searching for. Or perhaps (as is so often the case with an impulsive plant purchase) you'll find an item you can't resist, then return home undecided about its place in your garden. Indeed, half the fun of such spontaneous purchases is the inevitable walk around the yard with the object in your hand, as you ponder where to put it.

Also consider an object's weather-worthiness. Those that were already outdoor residents, like wheels or heavy pots, can become permanent fixtures. But others—an attractive watering can, for instance—may have to assume their positions in milder weather and be removed to storage in the off-season.

The attraction of whimsical ornaments is that they give your garden its own special personality. Decorating your garden with fanciful objects is an act of playfulness and joy. From start to finish, it gives your gardening experience an extra dimension of adventure.

ABOVE: Some watering cans may be too ancient or too lovely to actually use, but they make enchanting garden ornaments. Utility—even if faded—is always beautiful in its own right. Set an unusual vintage can on a bench, atop a garden wall, or on a wide stairstep for a charming, natural-looking tableau.

OPPOSITE: Give some thought to color combinations when you include antique decor in your garden. Weathered wooden artifacts gain enchanting warmth in the company of red and bronze leaves and flowers.

ABOVE LEFT: An old galvanized metal watering can, complete with an imposing, hand-punched rose, looks right at home at the edge of a flower bed, as if the gardener was just taking a break and will be back shortly. When something this useful becomes decor, you suddenly realize how handsomely designed it is.

ABOVE RIGHT: Old machinery sometimes makes for whimsical garden decor. Oftentimes, the objects were sturdily built (thus ought to be able to weather outdoor conditions) and had attractive details that make them a handsome addition. They can also be conversation pieces, as your friends speculate what they were used for; this item, photographed in an English garden, is a "mangle," which squeezed excess water from laundered clothing and sheets.

OPPOSITE: If you can find one, an old millstone makes a wonderful garden ornament—once you lug it into position, that is, as they can be extremely heavy and unwieldy. Some gardeners convert the stone into a simple bubbling fountain.

ABOVE: Everything about this vintage fountain suggests languor and tranquility. The sunlight plays off the water's surface, moss blankets the crevices and edges, and the water bubbles and drips rather than making the big, dramatic splashes often associated with modern or formal fountains.

OPPOSITE: When you go shopping for fountains, you'll discover that the options are endless. Many are sleek and modern, but consider something old and full of character, like this theatrical elephant. His presence in a simple, shallow pool conjures evocative images of far-off lands.

LEFT: A creative landscaper saw an interesting opportunity in the arching shape and cross slats of a retired dory. Part of the prow is buried for stability, and a climbing vine has successfully been trained up the sides, integrating this whimsical item more firmly into the garden.

RIGHT: Birdhouses are a cottage industry; you can buy adorable ones from gardening catalogs, pick up rustic ones from roadside hobbyists, stumble across neglected ones in barn sales, or even make your own from salvaged materials. Even if birds never take up residence, a birdhouse in the garden offers pleasure enough with its diminutive charm.

ABOVE: Gazing balls have gone in and out of style. Advocates rhapsodize about the mirrored reflections of clouds, branches, foliage, and blossoms. The availability of quieter colors, such as this deep blue one, and non-traditional mounts and pedestals also argue for a fresh appraisal. The fact is, the presence of a thoughtfully placed gazing ball can be downright fanciful.

ABOVE: The ornamental wheelbarrow, here nearly overrrun with a rambling rose, is an idea perhaps inadvertently invented by a busy gardener who forgot to finish a planting job. A discarded wheelbarrow from a junk yard or garage sale will do the trick; you can skip the repairs if it is going to be permanently parked. You should, however, make some arrangement for drainage if none exists, so water doesn't pool around the roots after you water the plants.

ABOVE: A handcrafted ceramic jug, no longer in mint condition but certainly still useful and good-looking, occupies a secluded corner. The worn finish and old-fashioned spigot give it an appeal that makes you forget all about going to the hose.

ABOVE: Well-chosen ornaments bring immediate charm to an otherwise nondescript corner of the garden. Here, a restored lantern and stand are a beacon of interest. Its creamy slate color is different enough to be visible in the shade and against the green foliage, but complementary enough to blend in. Terra-cotta pots (one is a salvaged chimney pot) and a wire basket filled with rivers stones also add to the palette.

ABOVE: It's not a wheelbarrow—and closer inspection will surprise and delight visitors to the garden. The wheeled base came from an old baby carriage and the container is a washtub that happens to fit. The load of bountiful herbs and soil anchors it in place.

POTS AND CONTAINERS

Exhibit directors at art galleries and museums say that the frame is as much a work of art as the painting within. This is not always true, but perhaps there are times when it should be. Certainly, some thought and creativity should go into the pairing.

So it is with containers and plants—a fabulous, interesting pot or planter does much for the plants it bears. The pot presents, it frames, it flatters, increasing the significance of the plants it holds. An inspired combination of plant and planter elevates the garden it adorns.

Vintage containers are much in demand, which is understandable. Prowl flea markets, yard sales, and country auctions for interesting pieces that might be put to a new use. Like other garden antiques, old containers can be assumed to be durable. They'll show the effects of weather and water and wear over the years, but therein lies their special appeal. Who can resist the grand sense of history you get from a handsome old pot? Maybe it evokes a stately British mood, maybe a classic Mediterranean feel, or maybe even a period and a place much more ancient than that.

OPPOSITE: A bloom-drenched climbing rose drapes itself over an aged Pyrenean olive oil jar, conjuring up visions of ancient secret gardens, with olive orchards beyond their walls and solitude and rich fragrances within. Remember that you needn't fill a pot with plants to make it a part of the garden; often, a beautiful pot may stand alone as an art object and be viewed like a sculpture.

RIGHT: Terra-cotta pots planted with succulents are always attractive, but this display becomes especially captivating thanks to the imaginative use of an old washstand—something that might be had for a song at a junk shop. You might need to do a bit of repair or add some new parts, but resist the urge to clean up too much—a vintage item derives its charm from the very fact that it shows its age.

ABOVE LEFT: What to plant in a rustic, aged stone container? This gardener went for texture and color, matching the rough stone surface with the heavily marked leaves of Rex begonias. The result is a pairing that makes both partners look grander.

ABOVE RIGHT: Succulents, possibly more than any other plants, look at home in older pottery. Here, burgeoning echeveria inhabits a small planter; the glazed vessel and ornament alongside underline the feeling of antiquity as well as provide harmonizing color.

OPPOSITE: Stone basins with formal, still-sharp lines deserve regal placement and careful attention to plantings, both within and nearby. Equally important is taking into account the color of the stone. Maroon, green, and white flowers and foliage bring genuine elegance to this planter's cool, pearly hue. As in a traditional border, the low-growing plants are placed in the foreground, with taller varieties occupying the back—adapt the rules of design for your containers, keeping in mind their scale and the angles from which they'll be viewed.

ABOVE: These elegant tulips look stunning because the pot is so perfect. Note that it is about as deep as the flowers are tall, providing a sense of balance. And observe how the weathered, dampened cast cement, with its silvery hues, highlights the sparkle in the creamy-hued blooms above. The pot's color is neutral enough to blend into the surrounding vegetation, too. Indeed, this deceptively plain pot truly succeeds in achieving the coveted "always been there" look.

ABOVE: Stone looks just right in the corner of a small, formal garden. A more modern pot, of plastic or clay, would look somehow insubstantial or out of step with the stone terrace. Instead, the ornamental cast-stone pot blends effortlessly with the terrace floor and the accompanying bench. The container also acts as a nicely understated supporting player to the crisp red blossoms and two tones of foliage above, enhancing rather than clashing with the plant selection.

ABOVE: Here's an idea well worth borrowing. An ornate stone planter box elevated on two stone supports (which match, but really needn't) brings its charms closer to passersby. It is also easier to water and tend the plants. Had the planter been situated on the ground, it still would have been admirable, but the delightful pedestals truly raise the container to a new level.

ABOVE: Urns of metal, especially cast iron, are widely available. Because they don't fade or crumble, they have a commanding air—they speak of endurance in a changing setting. Classic urns bring various associations to mind, and these impressions can be encouraged by judicious siting; this is the sort of pot you might unearth in an overgrown New Orleans courtyard, a rambling English estate, or an otherwise modest upstate New York shade garden.

ABOVE: Copper is a soft and beautiful metal that ages gracefully; anyone who has containers made of it longs for the aqua patina, or verdigris, that appears over time. Get creative and incorporate the venerable color into your landscape. This pot has been daringly paired with chartreuse-hued *Euphorbia palustris.*

ABOVE: When moss coats a clay pot, your garden gains a wonderful sense of history. A well-used container inevitably achieves this look with prolonged exposure to moisture within and without, but you can speed the process along on a new clay pot by keeping it in a humid place (such as a greenhouse or bathroom) for a while or by spraying a solution of buttermilk on the dampened pot surface.

ABOVE: Jaunty cosmos and bright yellow dahlias fill this metal milk pail, adding extra color to the flower garden. Adorn picnic tables, porch railings, or quiet corners of the patio with jubilant arrangements in old-fashioned country pails or vintage water buckets, bringing the bounty of the garden to the areas where people are most likely to congregate.

RIGHT: Fun and intrigue abound in this whimsical Santa Fe garden, where painted walls and window frames consort with exuberant flowers and what appears to be a very old pot. Its uneven rim and shape indicate that it was hand-thrown and shaped rather than machine-turned; handmade pots, old or new, always have this distinctive feel, so be sure to seek them out when you go container shopping.

ABOVE: A worn but lovely bas-relief decorates this small lead planter; the gardener wisely planted for minimal foliage spilling over the sides, then set it away from other pots and plants so its beauty could be appreciated from all angles. The wide, shallow form is also a bit unusual, and looks well with the taller pots that decorate the background.

LEFT: Lions' heads and garlands ring this massive stone urn. When you find a planter in excellent condition, it is imperative that you site it so that its features are not hidden. Thus boxwood, a nontrailing plant, inhabits the pot proper, and the entire thing is situated in the open and elevated above the billowing perennials.

OPPOSITE: Lead containers are rare these days for various reasons, including their heavy weight. But if you happen upon one that you like and haul it home, be sure to choose a spot for it that seems permanent. This planter is shaped specifically for a corner, where it can settle out of the way and be decorated with waves of bright flowers.

Part Two

HANGING
BASKETS AND
PLANTERS

INTRODUCTION

*P*ossessing the wondrous ability to introduce garden touches practically anywhere, including high overhead, hanging baskets and planters open up a world of possibilities. Some plant lovers rely upon these features to extend their gardens to "untillable" areas. Others rely upon them because of space and time constraints. After all, these miniature gardens are less labor-intensive than, say, caring for a major perennial border. But they can be just as beautiful to behold and as satisfying to nurture. They also have the advantage of being more intimate—easier to see, touch, sniff, and appreciate daily.

This book is meant to jog your creativity. You will see lovely and unique plant choices, as well as exciting pairings of flowers and foliage. And the planters themselves come in all sorts of materials, shapes, sizes, and styles. Whether you prefer wood or stone, large or small, formal or casual, handcrafted or machine-made, the containers that best suit your needs are out there. Many even boast supporting hardware that is attractive in its own right. You might want to choose a planter that can be deftly integrated with such architectural features as a window, wall, or porch. Or you may simply opt for a scene-stealer—a container so original and stunning that it stops visitors in their tracks.

Whatever you do, have fun. Designing and putting out planters is like the theater. You can let the container be the star or have the plants within take center stage. You can replant or reposition. You can direct attention to highlights (or deflect attention from flaws) in your garden area. You can delight, surprise, and entertain.

With regard to caring for these diminutive gardens, make sure that there are drainage holes, and water often, especially in warm weather. Fertilize regularly because the plants will quickly deplete whatever nutrients were originally in the soil mix. If the plants get lanky, cut them back and wait for a fresh flush of growth. If leaves or flowers are sparse, and you are otherwise providing good care, chances are the planter is in need of a sunnier spot. In the end, you will agree that tending to these small gardens is easy and highly gratifying.

OPPOSITE: What makes this balcony so irresistible is the color scheme. The gardener has chosen plenty of different plants and pots, and varied means of displaying them, but has stuck to a unifying theme of yellow and red.

ABOVE: A wall pot basically looks like half of a regular container, with a flat surface to go flush against the wall. Obtain the anchoring hardware from the same supplier, and hook the configuration to the wall prior to planting, just to make sure it holds. Then remove the setup, and fill it with lightweight potting mix and a few plants. As they begin to grow, the plants will hide the supports from view and make for a pretty picture. The gardener here has selected a pot with a painted-on flower that resembles the blooms planted within.

ABOVE: The principles often used in putting bouquets together can also be applied to window boxes. Observe how the bright orange and yellow nasturtiums sit in the center, flanked by modest red, pink, and white flowers. To round off the arrangement, the sides are gathered together by sprays of small purple lobelia blooms. The result is balanced, interesting, and attractive.

ABOVE: A window with green trim will flatter any color of flower. Here, a white curtain inside offers a clean backdrop, its delicate fabric echoing the softness of the petals. Matching tones are provided by the broad geranium foliage and the flowing white lobelia. The pinks and purples, though, immediately grab the eye.

ABOVE: This beauty is so laden with blooms that the basket is completely hidden from view. But it was not so at the outset; the gardener has surely encouraged the prolific show by keeping all the plants well watered and coaxing them along with regular doses of fertilizer. All in all, this is really not much effort to expend for such a fabulous display. And if your space is limited, just one basket like this can be your pride and joy.

ABOVE: Yellow oncidium orchids flash like sunbeams from shadowy tree branches. The plain, wood-slat container is practical because orchid roots need excellent drainage and ventilation, but the receptacle also acts as an understated supporter, deftly blending in with the bark of the tree. All attention is directed where it should be—to the radiant tiers of yellow.

ABOVE: Gardeners weary of winter and eager for spring start their containers early. Here, such favorites as 'Tête-à-tête' daffodils and snowdrops burst into bloom above a complementary mound of variegated ivy. The iron hanger and metal chain provide the support needed for the rather bulky basket.

ABOVE: Small pots can be attached to fences or trellises with sturdy clips, available at some garden centers and in various specialty nursery catalogs. Here, such clip and pot combinations are full of bright primulas, which should keep blooming for many weeks, especially in cool, early spring weather. The wall behind the cheery display has been treated with a green finish to provide a subtle, natural-looking backdrop.

RIGHT: A porch gains privacy with the help of fully packed planters. In fact, the barrier is now nearly twice as high, thanks to the purple petunias and delicate white blooms. While most of the sitting area is shielded from prying eyes, people relaxing on the porch are still able to take in the surrounding scenery.

ABOVE: A recessed window benefits greatly from a heavily planted box. In such a situation, the flowers should be bright enough to burst forth from the shadows. And, as in the landscaping of shade areas in the garden proper, plants with variegated leaves, such as these ivies, work particularly well. Note how the texture of these leaves echoes that of the stone surface.

ABOVE: Do you have a wall that is cloaked in green ivy? Before the window gets lost to view, put in a window box and fill it with billowing, bold-colored flowers, such as these red petunias. Red geraniums or begonias, or any other candidate with large flowers, would also do the trick.

ABOVE: A low stone wall with a broad, flat top can be an ideal place upon which to rest a container. Just make sure that the vessel is heavy and sturdy enough to stay where you set it. No wind or summer storm is likely to dislodge this massive stone urn. You should also plant enough in the container to achieve a show on all sides, for the ensemble will surely be an attention-getter for anyone coming or going. In this somewhat shady spot, the gardener has wisely used plenty of shade-loving tuberous begonia plants, accented with trailing ivy.

RIGHT: A balcony in the sun is a perfect spot to grow herbs. Here, basil and parsley (both curly-leaved and flat-leaved) thrive in a decorative planter. The container is small enough to hang comfortably on the railing, but large enough to support the herbs' growth. Creating a powerful sense of harmony, the designs on the planter echo the pattern on the railing.

RIGHT: The edge of a porch abounds with excitement, thanks to a planter filled with boisterous, somewhat unorthodox plant choices. Opening their faces up to the sun, eager 'Plaisir' tulips can't help but bring a smile to those they encounter. These flowers' bare stems are hidden by horned violets (*Viola cornuta*) and tufts of *Saxifraga × arendsii*, which weave smoothly in between to tie everything together. Bulbs are easy to grow in a container as long as they are buried several inches below the soil mix's surface. Reminiscent of a picket fence, the blue planter sets a traditional tone.

ABOVE: Broad, shallow steps and a low wall practically beg for the adornment of containerized plants. Using clay pots to match the bricks is a nice touch, and repeating the same flowers, or at least the same colors, from one pot to the next supplies a unified feel.

ABOVE: Do you have a lot of space to cover? Think big and think repetition. A progression of large pots is certainly up to the job. Since such vessels offer room for plenty of soil, generous plantings are possible.

HANGING BASKETS

A hanging basket that displays a little extra creativity can revitalize part of your home's exterior or a corner of your yard. Indeed, it can make all the difference in the world. Where once was a lackluster spot, now hangs something unexpectedly beautiful.

So seize the opportunity. Don't settle for a pedestrian green plastic basket, preplanted, purchased haphazardly at a local market—a basket that you bring home only to find doesn't fit in with your landscape. Instead, choose the location first and prepare the container second. Is the spot you have in mind shady for most of the day? If so, find out which plants prosper in shade; vivid tuberous begonias are a splendid choice, as are imaginative combinations of various foliage plants or fragrant herbs. Perhaps your targeted site is a small nook that is barren of color. Then compose something cheerful and vivacious to bring the area to life.

If you don't expect the plants to cover the container, choose a basket that's decorative. There are many different kinds of hanging baskets, as well as pots that can be rigged to hangers. Plastic containers are light and practical, and a little hunting can turn up a rainbow of color choices. Other options run the gamut from wire baskets, lined with sphagnum moss, to unique handcrafted ceramic containers.

Remember that a pot full of soil mix and plants, watered, can be heavy. This will be a factor not only on the first day as you endeavor to hang your creation, but also in the weeks to come. The pot must be sturdy, and the supports appropriately strong. The overhead hook or hanger must also be up to the job.

One last practical note: give some thought to how high or low you want the basket to hang. Too high, and not only will it be difficult to care for, but few people will be able to admire it properly. Too low, and you run the risk of creating an obstacle rather than a lovely decoration!

ABOVE: There's something thrilling about this small basket of ordinary geraniums. Poised daintily overhead, it exudes an air of simple elegance. The design of the wooden container echoes the lines of the house, while the scarlet flowers burst onto the scene to supply rich color.

OPPOSITE: The theme of pink, with its many variations, has been used to create a memorable feast for the eyes. Tutulike blossoms of fuchsia and some bright geraniums steal the spotlight, but a supporting cast of soft-hued lobelia and shell-pink petunias graciously provides backup.

ABOVE LEFT: Common plants—lobelia, petunias, begonias, daisylike bidens—are made uncommon when combined artfully in a hanging planter. This gardener chose primary colors to make the displays as clean and bold as possible against the pale hues of the house.

ABOVE RIGHT: Petunias used to be bedding plants only, and they were so frequently employed that most people became blind to their charms. Then, not too long ago, breeders developed petunias with trailing habits (and somewhat smaller flowers). These have turned out to be terrific hanging basket candidates, thanks to their compactness and propensity to bloom like gangbusters. They are also fairly drought-tolerant, so they can weather some neglect and still look great. Shown here is 'Hot Pink'; another favorite is 'Purple Wave'.

OPPOSITE: With its soft green hues and lush nature, *Helichrysum petiolare* appears to be a favorite of the gardener residing here, for it has been planted in the ground, as well as in the overhead baskets. This echo effect is a good plan if you garden in a limited amount of space and want to create the illusion of bounty.

ABOVE: Imagine how static this scene would be without the pair of hanging baskets, whose bold red and white flowers inject welcome exuberance. By placing one basket over each bench, the gardener maintains the symmetrical composition of the hardscape, allowing the plants to live in harmony with the setting. The whiteness of the hangers is a finishing touch that ties all the elements together. Notice how the baskets are hung high enough overhead that they won't interfere with someone sitting below.

ABOVE: The close quarters of baskets have their advantages. As blooms spill over each other and weave into each other's "territories," color combinations become compressed and intimate. Thus, you won't be left wishing that the purple centers of the trailing petunias would call out the purple of the lobelia—they will.

ABOVE: Here's a basket with an innovative theme: colorful leaves. This artful mix includes ivy, its leaves splashed with cream, and *Carex* 'Evergold', a yellow, grassy sedge, which is fronted here by the variegated form of *Hakonechloa macra*. Red-leaved *Tellima* and yellow-flowered *Epimedium* also chime in, while pink-spiked heather (*Calluna* 'Silver Knight') sprays out behind. All of these are durable plants that keep their color for a long period of time, well into autumn. Clearly, a fair amount of effort went into assembling and planting this exciting basket, but the gardener is rewarded with easy maintenance and splendor.

ABOVE LEFT: Who says hanging baskets belong only on the porch? Here, suspended from a sturdy tree branch, a great show of pink trailing verbena infuses the surroundings with radiance. These flowers can go outdoors once temperatures begin to rise in early summer, by which time the tree blossoms will have passed and the new addition of color will be much appreciated.

ABOVE RIGHT: Clematis in a basket? We usually think of these big-flowered beauties as rangy vines that are ideal for mounting trellises. But this clematis, 'Silver Moon', works well here, as it is one of a handful of cultivars with an especially compact habit.

OPPOSITE: Moss-lined baskets not only add a natural-looking touch to your garden, but also provide excellent drainage for the plants grown within them. The moss acts as a reservoir, soaking up extra water and releasing it back into the soil mix as required. A little evaporation also takes place, increasing the local humidity. Such conditions are bliss for almost any plant, save succulents. Here, an arresting display is achieved as the flowers make their way through the openings of an intricate sphere.

LEFT: The rules change when it comes to container gardening. Creeping Jenny (*Lysimachia nummularia*) is such a rampant grower that most gardeners view it as a pest; however, in a hanging basket, it eagerly provides lush tresses of yellow blooms that you can count on. Similarly, red valerian (*Centranthus ruber*) is considered troublesome, as it often self-sows into spots where it is not wanted. Confined, though, it pumps out a continual supply of beautiful reddish flowers.

ABOVE: Lobelia—in blue, purple, or even pink or white—is a favorite edging plant, valued for its prolific flowering and agreeable nature. The trailing varieties are ideal for basket life, as they will quickly cascade over the side of a pot for a sumptuous and dependable display. Here, they adorn a cabin entrance and enhance the home's natural look.

LEFT: A traditional hanging ivy basket has been enhanced by the imaginative addition of ami-able companions. A mound of ajuga, with its mottled leaves, adds a splash of color, while dense-growing lavender cotton (*Santolina chamaecyparissus*) con-tributes texture. The whole ensemble dresses up the white porch and brings those relaxing there one step closer to nature.

RIGHT: At the other end of the same porch, a basket of blooms hangs overhead, which just goes to show that containers lined up in a row don't have to sport the same plants for a harmonious effect. The symmetry of the scene is maintained by the placement of each basket beside a chair, while welcome variety is provided by the different colors and textures.

ABOVE LEFT: It is hard to say where the flowers planted in the ground end and the ones tumbling down from the suspended baskets begin. If a riot of color is your wish, this approach is definitely worth imitating. Just be sure to hang the baskets far enough out from the wall that you'll still be able to reach them for grooming and watering.

ABOVE RIGHT: The most striking hanging basket in this picture is the one at the top with the surprising plants—tomatoes and parsley. The tomato planted here is the cultivar 'Tumbler', which sports a naturally trailing habit. The parsley, a curly-leaved type, is a mound-former. Together, they charm the eye and entice the palate.

OPPOSITE: Solid brick and straight lines are immediately softened by a few hanging baskets. Note how the plants have been allowed to go a bit wild, billowing out over the confines of their pots. Together, they turn a staid setting into an inviting one.

WINDOW BOXES

They may be small in size, but window boxes can certainly have a big impact. Their very presence transforms otherwise unused, uninteresting spots into gardens. Suddenly, there's life and color. Passersby will smile and pause to admire. Butterflies and hummingbirds might pay a visit if the plants you've chosen offer the nectar they love. Even people inside the house will enjoy glimpses of the display.

For some, such as apartment dwellers and other people with limited space or time, window boxes may provide the only opportunity to garden. Fortunately, window boxes can be fabulous showpieces, and the plants they contain can present a jaunty, even heroic bid for beauty. And you don't even have to use an actual window box. An array of pots on a sill can create quite the stir.

Although many think of window boxes as simply garden accents, attention to the plants and containers is still important—and rewarding. Perhaps you will want to create a color union between the flowers, the planter, and the outdoor furniture below. Or perhaps the paint treatment or architectural style of the window frame, sill, or shutters will provide the opportunity to create what is essentially a little vignette.

In any event, assure the success of your window box by making sure it is securely mounted so it can bear the weight of the contents. Provisions for water drainage are also key, so roots won't be subject to rot. Speaking of water, don't forget regular applications; window boxes tend to dry out surprisingly quickly. You may be able to reach the display from inside the house with a long-necked watering can, or from outside with a hose or watering wand.

A garden on this scale is easy to nurture and can be both cozy and lovely. And remember, the window that opens to flowers is truly a joyous place.

OPPOSITE: Geraniums are unique in that they come in a number of different forms, which you may combine if you so desire. Close inspection of this window box reveals that those in the center are regular bedding-plant geraniums, while the ones skirting the perimeter are ivy geraniums.

RIGHT: Painted walls and a colorful blue shutter issued a challenge for window gardening here. The dilemma was whether to include plants that matched the blue, the yellow, or the pink—or a combination. The decision to go with pink, the hue gracing the areas closest to and farthest away from the window, has caused the whole wall to be included in the viewer's impression. Thus, a tiny garden seems somehow larger.

LEFT: Spring is greeted in style with this sprightly window box, filled to the brim with pristine, white blooms. The monochromatic theme is jazzed up by the use of a variety of flowers, all of which contribute different looks and textures to the mix. Creamy daffodils tower above fragrant hyacinths, while spotless primulas and white-bordered ivy rest at their feet. In cool weather, this display will continue to look handsome for up to two weeks. When warmer weather arrives, everything except, perhaps, the ivy may be removed to make way for another seasonal show.

ABOVE: Bright white paint and a dark window are joined by pansies that mimic the effect; the flowers' interiors are dark and their edges white. Demure, unremarkable pots graciously house the flowers, but in no way detract from their shining performance.

OPPOSITE: Sitting pretty in the window, pink and red geraniums jump out against the pale beige and tan hues of the home's exterior. To keep the setting as colorful as possible, the gardener has set pots with more geraniums and some perky yellow and orange marigolds along the ground below. Carved architectural details on either side of the window cleverly extend the floral theme.

RIGHT: Cast-iron grates, often mounted over city windows for security reasons, are not easy to work with. A bold shout of color, as provided by these big-blossomed geraniums, is an inspiring choice. No longer is this window forbidding; indeed, it now looks like a handsome framed picture. The rectangular band of detailing at the bottom of the grate creates the illusion of a window box, even though the flowers really reside in a clay pot.

LEFT: You don't have to decorate a windowsill with colorful flowers. These elfish topiaries, in their handsome terra-cotta pots, form a bewitching vignette without help from any blooms. The symmetry of the composition and the way in which the plants are framed by the architectural trim establish a serene sense of order, but the jauntiness of the clipped plants exudes charm.

ABOVE: The exterior of a traditional-style building is greatly enhanced by a formal window box exhibit. Rising from a carpet of ivy and prostrate juniper is a diminutive, smiling urn planted with a fountain of slender-leaved sedge (*Carex* 'Sunshine'). In attendance are some compact-growing heaths (*Erica gracilis*) and coralbells (*Heuchera* 'Rachel'). Adding another type of container to a window box is an innovative idea, worthy of imitation if you can work the container into your composition so that it is neither too prominent nor overwhelmed.

ABOVE: Primary colors arise from a thickly planted window box on a narrow sill. All are harbingers of spring: tulips, grape hyacinths, primroses, and violas. To keep such an array looking its triumphant best for at least several weeks, fertilize every time you water (mix the plant food at half strength with the water) and pinch off any petal, flower, or leaf that isn't holding up to the rest of the show.

OPPOSITE: Herbs crowd a terra-cotta planter, shown off to good advantage by a comely lace curtain. From left are lavender, rosemary, sage, basil, parsley, and fennel, with a few flowers brought in for color. Herbs like to grow in clay containers; while they do need water to prosper, they don't care for soggy soil, and porous clay naturally wicks away excess moisture.

ABOVE: If you are lucky enough to inherit or find a window tray support that is this attractive, don't obscure it by plunking a window box on top of it. A few simple pots will highlight the charms of this prized feature. Here, pots made of terra-cotta stand out solidly against the white architectural trim and gauzy curtains while picking up the tones of the brick wall. To match the elegance of the support's swirling vine design, the gardener has chosen a group of formal-looking plants for the setting. The middle plant is a dwarf flowering hydrangea, which is flanked by small pieris plants.

OPPOSITE: Any gardener who willingly plants yellow loosestrife (*Lysimachia punctata*) knows he'll have blooms in abundance. So a profuse window box in the area is appropriate to complete the impression of bounty—and wildness. This planter has been given over entirely to a purple-flowered oxalis. The whole arrangement keeps the eye engaged at all levels.

PLANTERS FOR WALLS AND FENCES

The wish to decorate every available nook, cranny, corner, railing, and surface of an area with plants is a passion. It is also a lot of fun. And there are many creative ways of filling these spaces with the foliage and blooms that you love.

Granted, walls and fences are frequently the bare spots of any garden, valued more for their utility than for their aesthetics. They define boundaries, enclose your sanctuary, and provide privacy. But there's no reason you can't also use them to add an extra measure of color and beauty.

Since walls and fences obviously cannot provide soil on their own, you must adorn them with pots or baskets of some sort. There are numerous clever ways to attach planters to the targeted surface. The necessary hangers and screws can be purchased wherever a wide selection of containers is available. And if all else fails, or if you simply prefer, you can just scoot a pot or two up close to the structure.

One advantage containers have on these vertical tableaus is that they are removable, and hence portable. Obviously, you could fill the same empty area with a flowering vine, an espaliered fruit tree, or a crush of flowers. But what if the plant doesn't prosper in that location? What if it looks plain or downright unappealing when it is not blooming or fruiting? Or what if your selection is simply slow to fill in its assigned space? With containerized plants, all you have to do is simply shift around the ones that aren't living up to their potential. Plus, you can change the contents of the containers as your whims and the seasons dictate. In the end, you'll get a display that you can rely on—right where you want it.

OPPOSITE: A vast brick wall is certainly monotonous to the eye, but what are your options? This gardener brought color to the scene by erecting a large trellis. Such a frame must be both strong enough and deep enough to hold all the flowerpots. It also needs to be attached securely to the wall so that the accumulated weight doesn't topple it.

RIGHT: An airy wrought-iron shelf is warmed by the addition of pelargonium ivy and purple flowers. If you include candles in the mix, make sure that the plants are far enough away from the flames that no leaves—either on the plants or falling off them—will catch on fire.

ABOVE LEFT: A small portion of a wall is transformed into a garden microcosm, thanks to a compact array of potted plants and a soothing fountain.

ABOVE RIGHT: Imagine this scene without the eye-catching pot of flowers. The leafy plants—hosta below the wall and euonymus above—would seem to recede into the shadows. The soft pastel hues of the blossoms are an inspired choice because they not only brighten the corner but also provide refreshing contrast against the heavy-looking brick wall.

OPPOSITE: Resting on a brick ledge with an imposing wall in the background, bleeding hearts (*Dicentra spectabilis*) are a welcome sight. The weathered lead trough not only enhances the garden's charm but also echoes the texture of the wall.

ABOVE: Wall sconce containers are swiftly gaining popularity. Fashioned to be attached to walls or fences, they make endearing planters. Heat-tolerant plants, such as this pink verbena 'Aphrodite' and the accompanying herbs, thrive in these setups because walls capture and reflect warmth.

RIGHT: Slim wall-mounted containers bearing marigolds enhance the quaint look of this country dwelling. The wraparound design of the attaching hardware creates the impression that the plants are being lovingly embraced. Plus, the fluid curves echo the rounded shapes of the leaves and flowers.

OPPOSITE: The vine may blanket the wall well, but it is not in bloom for long. Thus, the gardener has wedged in a number of pots on a narrow ledge to pick up the slack. They're filled with such long-blooming, easygoing annuals as alyssum, pansies, and petunias—plants that can be counted on to keep the spot colorful. If you have a similar situation in your yard but lack the helpful ledge, try tucking in a few tall, slender plant stands or supports.

RIGHT: Myriad flowers spring forth joyously from every inch of a narrow walled-in garden bed. This lush abundance was achieved with the help of hanging baskets displayed all along the wall.

ABOVE: For added pattern, try affixing pots to a trellis. Here, a once barren passage has been transformed into a verdant little garden. The stronger the trellis is, the more potted plants it will be able to exhibit.

RIGHT: A staggered arrangement of terra-cotta pots filled with marigolds and pansies enlivens a garden wall. The decision to use terra-cotta, which blends in with the naturalistic wattle background, allows the flowers to be the main focus of attention. The purple and gold color scheme is continued in the plantings below, creating a unified look.

LEFT: Visitors are warmly greeted at this doorway by a simple but utterly endearing basket stuffed with pansies. Better than a bouquet, the display of these durable little flowers lasts for months. The shape of the basket is reminiscent of a cornucopia, suggesting abundance.

ABOVE: A dim, uninteresting junction in a plain stone wall is made more intimate in scale and much more attractive with the addition of this planter. The white of the planter itself and the distinctive white cyclamen within dramatically brighten the scene; the variegated ivy also helps.

LEFT: There's something so spontaneous and playful about this old tin pail, casually hooked over a fence post and stuffed with flowering plants. It's as if the gardener scooped up the discarded pail and filled it on the run, temporarily placing it in a sunny spot. If your garage or basement doesn't yield any such containers, try a yard sale; there is much satisfaction and pleasure to be gained from rescuing such a castaway and giving it new life in your garden.

LEFT: If there's a wall or railing outside your kitchen, try growing some flowers in retired old pots and pans for a culinary theme. Since these cooking tools don't have drainage holes, the flowers will be better off if you plant them in a plastic pot that does, and then set them inside the pan. Surplus water can then be poured off easily.

RIGHT: Well-worn shoes nailed to the side of an entrance and filled with soil and plants create a whimsical and humorous diversion. With the shoes pointed downward and the plants growing up toward the sky, a riveting tug-of-war effect is achieved. Of course, part of the fun is encountering something on a vertical surface that we expect to see on a horizontal one.

CONTAINERS FOR DECKS AND BALCONIES

If your gardening area is a deck, balcony, porch, or patio, don't feel deprived. There are more opportunities than you might realize for growing and displaying plants in such spaces. Innovative hangers, attractive containers, and all sorts of plants can enhance these settings.

Think about what you want. If a sense of complete enclosure is what you're looking for, then cram in as many pots as you can, and let their plants spill out and over and into one another. Maybe you'd prefer just enough decoration to obscure straight lines or dull surfaces. To achieve this effect, begin conservatively, setting out just a few planters or pots at first and adding more only if necessary.

If you are fortunate enough to have a deck or balcony with a great view, choose garden elements that don't clamor for attention—perhaps a few undecorated clay, plastic, or wooden containers filled with plants known for their handsome foliage. Don't forget that potted plants allow you to move, add, and delete with impunity, so you can always alter your display until it satisfies you.

While making the most of limited space is challenging, it is also rewarding. When flowers and trailing foliage dress up a confined spot, you will enjoy retreating there. Just be sure to leave a place to sit and savor the fruits of your efforts.

OPPOSITE: Hardly any space, hardly any light, yet look at what the gardener has accomplished. A variety of textured surfaces captures interest and makes the tiny area seem larger. A sculpted head, made of terra-cotta like the pots, adds a stylish aura of antiquity.

RIGHT: Planters that blend with the deck's surface, as well as with each other, can set the stage for a quietly beautiful display. When you have troughs and pillars as attractive as these, you'll want to prevent the plants from overtaking them—so keep those clippers handy.

ABOVE: One large, dramatic pot can set the mood in a confined area. If you are able to select plants that mesh with the colors on the container—as these variegated-leaved geraniums do (plain old geranium leaves would never have the same effect)—the resulting combination will stimulate the senses.

ABOVE: The lushness of this area is achieved through a common trick—but it works. Fill a number of pots, then arrange them in a stepped manner so that you create the sensation of great height in a limited amount of space (use shelves, chairs, cinder blocks, or even an old stepladder). Grow compatible plants—here, primarily orchids and ferns have been used—to establish harmony.

ABOVE: When you don't have much gardening space, devote your efforts to a full, varied pot display and lavish it with water and fertilizer. The edge of a deck is a wonderful spot for showing off such a labor of love.

ABOVE: Classic architecture is spiced up with a refreshing sense of spontaneity provided by an informal planter on a porch railing. Framed perfectly by the window, the planter projects the illusion that it is actually a window box. The lively and airy array of flowers seems to spill out a genuine welcome to all who pass.

ABOVE: To take advantage of every precious inch, a gardener has placed pots at all different levels on this balcony. A few folk-art decorations, namely the duck, rooster, and birdhouse, pop up throughout the display, heightening the charm of the busy garden.

ABOVE: Even under a light dusting of snow, pots can do much to dress up or disguise a low railing. However, if your winters are quite cold and snowy, it's better to empty the pots and bring them inside. Otherwise, freeze-and-thaw cycles may cause the terracotta to crack—not to mention the fact that the plants' roots will freeze. These small evergreens (among them a dwarf fir and a miniature spruce) are pretty tough, though.

ABOVE: Containers have made possible this gardener's dream of a bountiful, verdant sanctuary. By placing grasses and trees in planters, the gardener has allowed the surrounding greenery to advance onto the patio.

ABOVE: Owners of wooden decks frequently employ wooden planters. Thus, the use of metal containers serves up a refreshing surprise. The neutral silvery shine and clean smoothness mesh easily with the surroundings while at the same time drawing attention to the sprays of ornamental grasses within.

ABOVE: Bouquets are always welcome on tables indoors, but when you have outdoor tables, go for living, blooming plants, such as these vibrant crocuses. Even a small table on a balcony can support such a display. And in many instances, calling upon the service of a decorative table, such as this tiled one, yields more impressive results than using a traditional plant stand.

LEFT: When space is at a premium, creativity is in order. How about decorating a garden bench with potted plants? Since the seat was most likely made to support a fair amount of weight, you can feel free to load it up. Here, large tubs of hyacinths mingle with terra-cotta pots of daffodils. As spring turns to summer, you can discard these plants and replace them with new bloomers.

ABOVE: All the care that went into choosing containers and pots has paid off in this tiny spot at the edge of a patio. Spiky grape hyacinths (*Muscari*) and chubby yellow ranunculuses flourish in pots at ground level, while a terra-cotta cherub serves up a generous arrangement of tulips, pansies, and more ranunculuses, bringing these flowers to new heights.

ABOVE: A daring idea, but it works. A large pot full of arching flowers, most notably pink-and-white bleeding hearts (*Dicentra spectabilis*), sits prominently atop a pedestal, enhancing the view from the porch. If you try this, make sure that the stand or table is out of the way of direct traffic, so that it won't be toppled accidentally. A corner of a balcony or patio would be an ideal spot.

RIGHT: Deck gardens benefit greatly from at least one
spectacular potted display.
Choose a large pot, and pack
it with exuberant growers.
The favored formula is to sit-
uate one or two tall plants,
preferably with spiky flowers
or sprays of leaves, in the center and surround them with
flowers that trail gently over
the sides.

Part Three

GARDEN GATES AND ARCHES

INTRODUCTION

✦

A gate is the threshold of a garden. It is a doorway to a sanctuary, a border between the world out there and the world in here, an invitation, a beginning to a story. If you are poised to install a garden gate, stop and ponder your choice with great care. The decision is an important one, as this feature will have a powerful effect on both the demeanor and practicality of your garden.

The right gate expresses a garden's character. This entrance should be in harmony with not only the fence it may be a part of, but also the plants beyond. An old-fashioned white picket gate promises an informal setting or a quaint cottage garden. A more contemporary design, perhaps fashioned from metal or sleek cedar, hints at exciting, nontraditional plants and ideas.

Naturally, a gate is meant to be functional. It should comfortably admit you and your guests, plus any gardening equipment you favor—from an ordinary wheelbarrow to a rototiller or riding mower. You might also want the gate (and an accompanying fence, arch, or arbor) to be a physical barrier against noise and intruders, animal as well as human. While see-through gates may seem inviting, they can also constitute a security risk that you may not be willing to take. In any event, it is generally best if your gate swings inward, keeping it in the domain of the garden and—most importantly—leading arrivals inside.

Your choices in the realm of gates are many. Instead of the traditional wooden or metal gate, you might consider an open entrance, which often takes the form of an archway. Such an entry deftly combines frankness with mystery. And the now-popular arbor and gate sets allow the entrance to become part of the garden itself.

The following pages not only present a vast range of gate options, varying in terms of style and material, but also show how these features can be seamlessly incorporated into different types of gardens. So go forth and choose well!

ABOVE: Red brick and clay dominate this courtyard, so the gardener wisely chose a dramatic contrast for the gate. The powder blue paint gives the eye a refreshing break from the reddish brown hues and prevents the area from seeming too oppressive. Left ajar, the little gate almost seems to spring open, graciously coaxing visitors to enter.

OPPOSITE: When the plant choices in a garden are not overly complicated, an intricate metal gate really lends a sense of style. Such a gate also works beautifully with gravel or flagstone-based courtyards, because the light hues of the stones throw the detailing into relief. The embellishment at the top of the gate is reminiscent of a peacock's feathers—a design that suggests the owners take great pride in their garden.

ABOVE: A garden with a casual, meandering layout is well served by an informal, trellislike gate. The gate's patterned design helps preserve the sense that a gardener's hand is at work here, while the rough, twiggy texture harmonizes with the plant life beyond. The natural-looking material echoes the slatted roof of the distant gazebo.

ABOVE: This archway of woven fibers introduces visitors to a temperate garden. Thanks to the material, the structure exudes a tropical air consistent with the plantings. Useful as well as atmospheric, the entry offers a patch of soothing shade and gracefully weathers outdoor conditions in the mild climate. Notice, too, how well the structure has been absorbed by its site; shrubs, vines, and palms have all been encouraged to embrace it from the sides.

RIGHT: Considerable effort went into constructing this arch, fashioned from pliant hazel stems in such a way as to give it a loose, carefree demeanor. Scarlet runner beans (*Phaseolus coccineus* 'Painted Lady') provide quick, easy coverage along the sides. Meanwhile, the upper portion of the bower is left bare to create a window to the treetops and sky. Owing to the fragility of the arch and the fact that the beans are perennial only in mild climates, this scheme is best emulated in areas with snowless winters.

ABOVE: When choosing a gate, it is often wise to consider what is inside and outside the garden. While this garden features a cultivated border of purple and yellow perennials, the area on the other side of the gate abounds with wildflowers. The white picket gate is a fitting choice, since it gives a similar impression of both order and informality. Moreover, the generous spaces between the slats allow visitors to enjoy the untamed beauty of the field from within the garden.

LEFT: Everything about this gate is alluring, from its open slat design, which filters sunlight and beckons visitors onward, to its crisp, bright whiteness, which glows against the dark hedge. Composed of two doors that are mirror images of each other, the gate echoes the striking symmetry of the plantings.

LEFT: When a garden seems more like an outdoor room, as is the case with this brick-lined courtyard, a gate that reminds one of the door to a home is a natural choice. This beauty features carved detailing that is a decorative equal to the formal purple blossoms of the potted agapanthus plant just inside.

ABOVE: Even in winter, the complete harmony of this landscape is apparent. From the picket fence and accompanying arch to the Adirondack chairs and the birdhouses of cabinlike design, the area has a rustic feeling. The arch not only marks the entrance, but also breaks up the repetition of the fence's lines.

ABOVE: Here is an outstanding example of an entryway carved out of a manicured hedge. As with any formal hedge, the gardener's clippers must be employed often during the growing season to maintain the outline and neatness of the design. But the extra effort is well worth it, as there is nothing quite like being ushered through such a majestic living portal. Tall, potted white tulips stand at attention on either side of the path to form an elegant receiving line.

OPPOSITE: Matching textures define this setting. The brick arch and brick path below it provide a common backdrop for a cheery array of flowers. This design scheme is especially useful for those who favor a wide variety of flowers in the garden yet feel that a unifying factor is desirable.

ABOVE: A strikingly modern gate made of metal panels greets visitors at a Swiss garden. The whimsically placed windows, which provide eye-catching views of hearty geraniums, banish any sense of exclusion and promise that the landscape within will be sunny and lively.

ABOVE: A metal gate can be every bit as charming as a wooden one. If it comes unpainted or looks too plain, spend a few hours trimming it. Just be sure to use a high-quality, glossy, weather-resistant paint intended for metal surfaces so that it will retain its luster for at least a few seasons. This playful gate pays homage to its more common counterparts with a colorful array of finials.

WOODEN GATES

The wooden gate is a garden icon—and with good reason. Many fences are made of wood, and it often makes sense to have the entryway composed of the same material as the rest of the structure. Wood also looks appropriate and natural; the wood that was once a tree is now a contributor to a planted landscape. And then there is the tactile element. Rough or smooth, painted or left bare, wood always feels solid, substantial, and durable. If you spring for expensive cedar, it even smells good.

Once you have decided on wood for your entrance, there are many options to consider, depending on your taste and budget. Redwood, cypress, and black locust are strong, decay-resistant woods, but they can be pricey and are not available everywhere. Pine and fir are softer, less expensive choices. Other possibilities include oak, Douglas fir, and hemlock. Visit a lumberyard to see what you like, even if you intend to install a manufactured gate.

Many woods weather over time, helping the gate, archway, or fence settle into the scene. The dove gray of aged cypress is especially handsome, imbuing the surroundings with a serene air. Of course, any wood's appearance can be enhanced, and its life extended, with wood preservatives, stain, or a coat of paint. One advantage to using paint is that this substance provides the opportunity to establish charming color vignettes with the flowering plants in the garden beyond. It also allows you to inject vital energy into an otherwise monotone setting. White is a classic choice that "goes with" everything, but what if you opted for periwinkle blue and grew a shell-pink rose next to the gate?

ABOVE: The sere, tan tones of an adobe wall and its attendant pottery are relieved by a vibrant shade of blue for the entrance. To keep the doors in harmony with the rustic surroundings, the gardener has allowed the paint to weather. Still, the hue retains its radiance and calls to mind the sea, hinting that a lush oasis lies beyond the threshold.

OPPOSITE: This casual picket fence–style gate presents something of a surprise, considering the formal company it keeps. Flanked by handsome clipped and trained greenery and approached by a classic flagstone path, the gate sports a coat of blue paint—another unorthodox touch for the setting. The design casts an air of intrigue, leading one to wonder if other tradition-breaking combinations await inside the garden.

ABOVE: An imaginative design can confer beauty and character on even the plainest wood. This gate's weatherbeaten, untreated timbers were the object of careful craftsmanship—note the smooth, symmetrical curves, the way the evenly set slats are neither too slight nor too thick, and the graceful effect of the neatly dovetailing lower boards.

OPPOSITE: Matching taller perennials, such as these phlox, echinops, and campanula, to gate height creates a powerful sense of accord. Wooden planking is a good choice because it does not clash with the flowers in terms of color or form—the unadorned, smooth surface looks great with everything.

ABOVE: A wooden gate—particularly a weathered one—is an ideal choice for an herb garden, as the aged appearance works well with plants that are rich in history and folklore. Here, the fossil designs foster the impression that both the gate and the freshly planted herb garden it protects have been around for eons.

OPPOSITE: If rustic appeal is what you desire, salvage sturdy old wood where you can and rig together the gate of your dreams. In this peaceful setting, the gate proves to be an agreeable companion for a wall of stacked stones bearing the same hues and unrefined demeanor as the wood. The enchanting cottage garden beyond is framed perfectly.

ABOVE: This gate acts as an effective link between the garden and the house, thanks to an invigorating coat of blue paint that matches the color of the window frames and mullions. The bold hue also provides welcome contrast to the pastel pink hollyhocks.

RIGHT: These big, blowsy rhododendrons would easily overwhelm the garden's entrance were it not for diligent pruning and a well-chosen gate. Despite the tightly packed blooms, the gate creates an airy feeling, thanks to its height, which is a good deal lower than the tall shrubs, and its generously spaced slats, which practically beg visitors to peek inside. With a sizable window of space between its base and the brick walkway, the gate appears to be floating magically.

ABOVE: Wider entries call for broader gates, and double gates prove to be an excellent solution. Dividing the entry space by using two doors helps retain a sense of intimacy. This handsome example includes heavy-duty posts, boards, and latch hardware, yet it never over-whelms, thanks to the double-door construction and see-through design.

ABOVE LEFT: Here, a double gate marks a vast entrance onto a sweeping lawn. The concave or "half-moon" top swings the focus toward the center where the gate opens and also cradles the view of the house beyond. In keeping with the rural setting, the lower portion of the gate resembles the styling found on many barn doors.

ABOVE RIGHT: When a garden brims with lavish greenery and carefully orchestrated perennial borders, an unpretentious wooden gate is ideal because it will quietly perform its service without competing with the surroundings. Here, such a gate is nestled beneath a bower of honeysuckle (*Lonicera*) and attended by rhododendrons. The overall scene makes you want to tiptoe in with a watering can or slip in early in the morning with a mug of hot tea.

ABOVE LEFT: An old stone wall with an archway requires a gate that not only fits the space but also varies the view. This wooden door fills the bill by supplying contrasting color and an open window to the landscape beyond.

ABOVE RIGHT: Here's a novel idea: the gate responds not so much to the plants as to the hardscape elements, from the café table and chairs to the rounded patio. Curves appear in the design of the gate, as well as in the individual split branches that make up the vertical slats. The feeling of being completely embraced by the garden is hard to resist.

OPPOSITE: Such cottage-garden favorites as wallflowers (*Cherianthus*) and forget-me-nots (*Myosotis*) billow around a slatted wooden gate. The gate's straight lines act as a strong foil for the flowing blooms, while the striking white color brightens up the commanding brick wall.

ABOVE: Many fences and walls in the American Southwest are constructed of thick, warm-colored adobe, made from indigenous clay. However, it is impractical to fashion gates from the same material. This gardener's solution is a wooden gate of deep, earthy brown that blends with the surrounding structure. By decorating all components—the wall, overhead arch, and door surfaces—with native images, the owner achieves an integrated whole.

ABOVE: This scene is a riot of textures and colors, with its brick pillars and pathway, the tan adobe wall, and the verdigris finish on the lantern-style lights, not to mention the exuberant growth of Shirley poppies (*Papaver rhoeas*). The worn wooden gate contributes to the excitement, presenting yet another surface and color to admire.

METAL GATES

There's just something so romantic, so classic, about a garden gate that is fashioned from metal. Whether of wrought iron, steel poles or panels, copper tubing, or a combination of these, a metal gate can be quite ornate and formal in creative hands. It also has the potential to project a modest and inviting appearance.

You can purchase a metal gate from a gardening catalog, garden-themed shop, or even some hardware stores. But if the gate does not need to be in mint condition, a salvaged one can be an exciting alternative. If you're lucky, you'll find a charming old one tucked away in some rural antique shop or at an estate sale. With a little cleaning and fixing, and perhaps some new latching or hanging hardware, a rescued gate can become a garden treasure.

Metal gates also boast the advantage of longevity—no rotting, no breaking down, no leaning. Looking like they have been solidly in place for ages, they endure the years stoically while the garden matures around them. Eventually, they may show some slight wear and tear, if only in a few dents or spots of rust—testimony to seasons of exposure and years of people and equipment passing through their portals. A coating of oil, oil-based or enamel paint, or a steel powder or galvanized finish will help sustain the surface.

ABOVE: Although a wide and substantial gate has the potential to be ungainly, this one bears a lacy design that gives it a delicate quality. The fanciful curlicues hide little of the garden, which tempts wanderers with its verdant scenery and flourishing blooms.

OPPOSITE: A gate of black forged-iron bars is an inspired choice for a garden whose most salient resident is a flowering cherry, because the trunk and branches of this type of tree are especially dark in color. Both the tree and gate gain a sculptural quality from their juxtaposition. Stone pots of produce perched atop the brick pillars hint at the delicious fruits of the garden.

175

ABOVE LEFT: Thanks to the mature trees and draping, flower-laden stems of the climbing rose, this garden appears to be well established. Yet the undisciplined growth of the gray-leaved lamb's ears (*Stachys*) and rosy-flowered valerian (*Centranthus ruber*) suggests that the gardener is not overly fussy or meticulous. The metal gate reinforces this relaxed sense of refinement with its clean lines.

ABOVE RIGHT: Formal settings call for formal gates. No wooden gate could ever provide the elegance that this metal entrance confers upon the sculpted elements within, from the regal stone pedestal to the highly refined, clipped boxwood and yew hedges in the distance. The darkness of the metal modestly keeps the focus on the garden itself, allowing the gate to retreat into the shadows.

OPPOSITE: Again, formal, dense hedges find a perfect mate in a dignified metal gate. This one sports an ebullient scroll design that displays a bit of whimsy, yet remains in keeping with the garden's stately character.

ABOVE: This classic, straightforward metal gate is actually no more than an extension of the fence. This type of setup works particularly well in a garden that is small or hemmed in by adjacent gardens. The fluid, no-nonsense design results in less distraction, thereby preventing the scene from seeming too busy.

OPPOSITE: Courtyards are well served by metal gates—the garden is still enclosed, but any feeling of confinement or claustrophobia is diminished. This gate bears a combination of curves and lines that creates the same airy impression as the transom above the front door. With its plain, solid posts and unpretentious design, the gate reflects the tone of the Japanese-style urban courtyard.

LEFT: A metal gate is a wonderful partner for a brick wall. Here, such a gate allows visitors to see in, as well as out, providing respite from the bricks' imposing nature. Upbeat alstroemerias in the foreground gain warmth from the coloring of the brick backdrop, even as they spring outward to meet those who enter.

OPPOSITE: A busy cottage garden, overflowing with roses and trellised sweet peas, is flattered by a dainty metal gate. While the gate's central pattern shares the lighthearted feeling of the garden's design, the frame consists of bold geometric shapes that imply the gate means business. The structure's airy styling helps open up the snug space, and its curving lines echo the delicate arms of the rose-colored bench.

LEFT: There is nothing terribly ornate or overbearing about this gate—nor is the design bluntly floral. Yet the way in which the metal pieces rise from the base and swirl upward and outward mimics the growth of the shrubs and flowers. The heart shape at the center of the composition extends a warm welcome and suggests that the garden is cherished.

RIGHT: This spare yet attractive iron gate is similar to the climbing rose it supports in that it boasts inherently elegant lines adorned with flourishes of beauty. Note that the arch is actually part of the frame and always remains solidly in place, providing stability for the roses so that they are not disturbed when the gate is opened. A flower design at the top keeps this garden in bloom year-round.

ABOVE: When you are installing a wall or fence at the same time that you are choosing the gate, you have the perfect opportunity to make a perfect fit. This situation is particularly beneficial when you are dealing with a metal gate, which cannot be whittled an inch or two here and there! This iron gate, painted white to give it an uplifting look, comes with its own metal arch to hang and swing from—a nifty way to ease the tricky problem of attaching hinges to stone.

ABOVE: A handsome wrought-iron gate emerges next to a billowing perennial border, bringing order and an element of constancy to the garden. The green lawn glimpsed beyond provides natural windows of color between the gate's black lines. Boosted by a stone step, the gate is slightly elevated, lending the garden an air of importance.

OPPOSITE: If you are enchanted by this gate, consider seeking out an enterprising metalsmith to forge one for your garden. You could even provide the old tools, salvaged perhaps from the garage, a junkyard, or an antique barn; they certainly don't need to be in working condition and probably shouldn't be sharp, for safety's sake. In the end, you'll have quite a conversation piece.

RIGHT: If your garden is less than colorful or the bloom time is relatively brief, a festive gate can fill the void. This handcrafted gate of folk-art design provides a point of interest and constant color throughout the seasons. Naturally, botanical themes work particularly well in this type of situation.

ABOVE: Note how the unadorned architecture of this gate secures the doorway without stealing the show from the decorative wall accents and the antique urn overhead. Planted with greenery, the urn allows the garden to become part of the entrance.

OPPOSITE: Mediterranean gardens go hand in hand with iron gates, which admit plenty of warm sunshine and breezes. This gate has the added advantage of slender bars and finial-inspired tops that echo the fan-trained vines mounting the wall. Tiles crowning the arch enhance the Mediterranean look and lend an air of distinction.

OPEN ENTRYWAYS

If you have adventurous taste and security is not a factor, consider an unorthodox choice: the gateless entryway. This type of passage is often an archway of some kind, and with careful consideration of the materials, placement, and adjacent plantings, it can be quite extraordinary.

The trick is to get such an entryway into place as early as possible in your garden's development. That way the structure can easily be incorporated or enveloped by the surrounding plants, and a harmonious environment can be achieved. If this strategy is not possible, you can clear a broad area, longer and wider than the proposed entry, and landscape the site anew. The success of the scheme rests on how well you are able to integrate the entryway with the garden. As many people find out the hard way, wedging an archway or the like into the midst of existing plants is not a particularly easy task.

Some entryways are composed entirely of plants, such as massive, twining vines or sculpted hedges. Others are pure hardscape, fashioned from brick, stone, wood, or other non-living materials. But an entrance that mixes these concepts, such as a rose-draped wooden arbor, is perhaps the most desirable. The support defines the opening, while the plant announces that a garden lies ahead.

ABOVE: This Japanese-influenced garden is approached through a graceful, moon-shaped entrance, which deftly frames the view and contributes to the overall theme of geometric shapes within the garden. The roundness of the entry has a nurturing effect, embracing those who pass through on their way to the peaceful setting beyond. Had an actual gate been installed in this opening, the flow would have been obstructed and the serenity lost.

OPPOSITE: As a stone path winds its way into the garden, a stone archway pitches in with a harmonizing note. To keep the massive entrance from seeming too imposing, the gardener has incorporated a delicate honeysuckle vine that provides a lighthearted touch of greenery and fragrance.

ABOVE LEFT: An intertwined grapevine and copper arch imbue this garden with a sultry feeling. The match remains beautiful throughout the seasons, as the leaves change from green to red to soft yellow against the metal's handsome finish. (Ultimately, copper left outdoors gains an appealing aquamarine patina, which alters the color combinations but is no less lovely.) A mural on the back wall tricks the eye into thinking that the cozy garden is much larger than it actually is.

ABOVE RIGHT: An archway of flowers is this gardener's idea of an inviting entrance. Since a climbing rose cannot be trained into this shape on its own, support is provided by stakes of willow, a strong but flexible wood. A rose with especially pliant canes is a wise choice for this type of setup. Here, repeat-blooming 'New Dawn' fills the bill.

OPPOSITE: The artistic hand of the gardener is evident here in every detail, from the dazzling path to the painted wooden beds to the daring color combinations in the flower borders. The entrance, too, transcends the ordinary with a copper arch whose bold stars suggest that there is something out of this world about the garden. Nestled in the midst of this celestial crown, the white petals of a popular clematis hybrid called 'Ernest Markham' provide heavenly accompaniment.

ABOVE: If the first tree a visitor will see is one that blazes with color each autumn, as does this sweet gum (*Liquidambar styraciflua* 'Worplesdon'), a brick entrance offers an ideal frame. With its warm red and rust tones, the archway sets the stage for the colorful show to come.

RIGHT: A pergola can achieve the magical effect of an outdoor "hallway." When the beams are cloaked in foliage and flowers, the resulting shade provides soothing respite from the hot sun. The extensive length of the entrance creates a feeling of suspense as to what the garden holds in store.

ABOVE: Young trees can be trained to form an archway. This technique, perfected in European gardens, is called "pleaching," from the French *plechier,* meaning "to braid." Linden (*Tilia*) trees are used here, but other options include beech (*Fagus*), hornbeam (*Carpinus*), and even apple (*Malus sylvestris*), all of which have sturdy, flexible branches.

ABOVE: This striking entrance gives one the sensation of peering through an oversize keyhole. The effect is tantalizing, offering a generous peek at the world beyond, while at the same time casting an air of intrigue.

ABOVE: Postcard pretty, this rustic vine-cloaked arch hails visitors at an ambitious British garden. An actual gate, even one with bars or slats to see through, would have interrupted the smooth flow from the front flower borders to the show within. No doubt the gardener must keep the foliage and flowers on the arch itself in control, so that the entrance remains accessible.

OPPOSITE: With its substantial depth and sheltering configuration, this dramatic stone structure is reminiscent of a foyer. Marking the transition into the garden's sitting area, the archway announces a shift in gears. The open design, as well as the trompe l'oeil vines climbing along the walls inside, ensures that the garden remains a strong presence at all times.

ABOVE: Filling the air with romance, a rose-laden arbor is difficult to resist. The profuse blooms and dense foliage showering this one suggest that the garden has been thriving for many years. However, this bewitching effect can be achieved in a mere season or two by planting a pair of husky roses and pampering them with water, fertilizer, and if necessary, sprays.

OPPOSITE: This dramatic arbor boasts a series of arches, large and small—a design that keeps the eye engaged. The encircling pink roses exude a celebratory tone, as though there were a lively garden party or wedding on the other side.

ARBOR AND GATE SETS

There is a growing trend these days toward buying and installing a gate that comes with a coordinating, overarching arbor. You can find these sets in a number of garden-supply catalogs and even at local nurseries that have sections devoted to garden decor. Generally, the structure comes unassembled, as a kit, complete with all the necessary hardware and detailed instructions. (Of course, if you don't feel up to the job, you can always get help from someone who is handy with construction projects.)

The advantages of these sets are many. Since the individual components are designed to go together, there's no awkward fussing and fitting—everything should snap neatly and sturdily into place. From an aesthetic point of view, they already work well together in terms of style, color, and proportion—with no effort on your part. And, last but not least, it is highly satisfying to erect a complete and beautiful garden entrance quickly.

But you don't have to go this route. You can make your own gate and arbor, or arch, set from plans you devise yourself or ones you find in a garden construction handbook (with modifications that suit your taste and your garden). Or you may be fortunate enough to find yourself with a garden that already has a gate or an arch, but not both, and decide to go ahead and put its mate into place.

One final note: a gate and an arbor or arch can be coordinated without bearing the exact same characteristics. A white wooden gate doesn't have to pair up with a white wooden arch, nor does a cast-iron gate require an arbor of the same material. After all, these structures are not operating in a vacuum. There is an entire garden to consider: plants already in place and those you intend to grow, pathways, and other hardscape elements. Peruse the examples in this chapter, take your cues from your garden, and install whatever seems right to you.

OPPOSITE: Echoing the home's framed doorway is this framed "outside doorway." Notice how the gate and arch combination permits the white climbing rose and other adjacent plants to grow freely without danger of their blocking the view. In a similar fashion, the entrance to the house plays host to casually draped pink blooms, while at the same time keeping the passageway easily accessible.

ABOVE: Here is a classic white wooden set, which you can buy as a kit and put together yourself. The color and style recall simpler times, when life was less hectic and time moved at a more relaxed pace. The setup, along with the calming view of the sea, sends the message that all worries and pressures must be checked at the door.

ABOVE: Since the tidy boxwood topiaries are meant to dominate this garden, the end of the allée is marked by a modest iron gate. But lest this feature be overlooked, a rose-covered archway has been added above it. The arch mimics the shape of the bushes and brings the entrance into scale with the garden.

OPPOSITE: This highly picturesque entrance is filled with wonderful touches. The concave gate meets with the overhead arch to form a vast, circular window into the garden. Emerald green accents artfully connect the man-made structure to the natural environment, while iron hardware adds a traditional flair.

ABOVE: This informal gate is made all the more friendly by the gingerbread-like design of the arch. The scalloped edges exude a fluid quality, creating the impression that they just might flutter gently in the breeze along with the leaves. The total picture makes you feel like bounding through the entrance to discover what treasures await in the garden.

LEFT: This entryway is a symphony of forms. Pointy, clipped evergreens echo the sharp finials on the fence, while an arch soars above them all in splendor. The ogee arch, topped by an abstract depiction of a tree, lends an exotic touch to the prim surroundings.

LEFT: While this hedge archway does not actually surmount the gate, it does deftly frame it. The setup elongates the garden's entrance, which is filled with a series of gradually descending steps. When designing the space, the gardener recognized the wisdom in simplicity and opted for a restrained, low wooden gate with slats to admit sunlight.

OPPOSITE: There was no better choice for this setting than a wooden gate, which maintains the natural look of the arching trees. The leafy tunnel (made of flexible hazel trees) selflessly extends shelter to those who pass through, causing guests to feel nurtured as they make their way to the garden. Note that the gate is not made of the same wood as the trees, but it works well because the thickness of its slats and supports is proportionate to the slender trunks.

ABOVE: In this enchanting design by landscaper Mirabel Osler, the arch and open gate provide a tantalizing glimpse into a sunny, flower-strewn setting. Even when the gate is closed, the alluring scene remains highly visible, thanks to the open crisscross pattern. The darkness of the wood makes the colors within the garden seem even more vibrant.

OPPOSITE: A birdbath and numerous low-growing plants are in good company with a low gate. The oft-used Z-construction is jazzed up by the inclusion of arching metal loops, which echo the shape of the clematis-filled arbor overhead.

ABOVE: A conventional Z-design wooden gate has met its match with a spare, geometric arch. Triangular in shape, the top of this arch is similar to the pediment of an interior doorway. The overall effect is decidedly "Western ranch," emphasized further by the addition of a period lantern.

ABOVE: The delicacy of this metal arch and gate set counterbalances the heaviness of the stone wall and the garden's dense box hedges. A climbing rose acts like a fine seasoning, preventing the entrance from seeming too bland by injecting a little zest. The overall effect is one of understated elegance, which ties in well with the formal setting.

RIGHT: Thick, lavish grapevines swoon over a bolstering wooden arch. The free-form design of the gate, composed of swirling branches, creates the illusion that this is not a gate at all, but rather a natural barrier of tangled growth.

Part Four

FOUNTAINS AND CASCADES

INTRODUCTION

*O*nce in a lifetime, if one is lucky, one so merges with sunlight and air and running water that whole eons, the eons that mountains and deserts know, might pass in a single afternoon....

—Loren Eiseley

Water in a garden always transforms it for the better, adding welcome notes of style, whimsy, solace, and magic. When the water is in motion, as with a fountain or cascade, the scene is alive and mesmerizing. And your sense of hearing—not usually awakened in a garden— is courted by the musical dance of water on water. On sunny days, droplets shimmer or glisten, playing with light in ways no plant or other object in your garden ever does. There is simply nothing quite like a fountain, and once you have installed one, you and everyone who visits will be completely captivated.

Any garden, from a formal estate to a modest suburban backyard, will benefit from a bubbling fountain. The space may be open and bright or green and shady—no matter the character of your plot, there is a suitable style for your garden. You can add a fountain to a planned pool, or with a little more effort, install one in or next to an already-present pool—in either case taking the display a step beyond the ordinary. Or consider clearing a space in a dull corner or other humdrum spot that until now has stymied your efforts to bring excitement or character. Your fountain can be the garden's focal point or it can be a hidden surprise.

This book will give you a tour of the range of fountains possible and show you how others have incorporated theirs into garden settings. Now you can dream of what your fountain will look like, what it will sound like, and how it will fit into the garden you already have or the one that you are currently composing.

So dream away, make your choice, and once your fountain is in place— relax at its side. For flowing water has the singular ability to envelop your senses, excluding all worries and cares; there is no sense of being confined, even in the smallest, tucked-away oasis or grotto. Fountains whisper, murmur, or exult, but their liberating, eternal message is a celebration of the life-giving force of water— truly, a waking dream.

ABOVE: Dome-shaped fountains are ideal for small spaces because the water's domain is so discrete and compact. Yet you still get the wonderful splashing sounds that make fountains such a joyful garden ornament.

OPPOSITE: The best fountains are in scale with their surroundings. Here, a tiny fountain gushing forth near a lilypad peeks out from a diminutive sunken tub, proof that even the most limited space can generate the bewitching sight and sound of splashing water.

LEFT: Taking a cue from European street fountains, this ingenious design combines a rock wall resembling the ramparts of a fine old castle with regularly spaced falling streams. The result is stylized yet utterly enchanting.

OPPOSITE: Matching the fountain, or fountains, to adjacent architecture is an exciting idea; the juxtaposition of static structure (in this case, the arched windows to the side and rear) and moving water creates a garden picture that resonates. The visitor might not notice right away if standing at a different vantage point, so make the best viewing spot obvious and accessible.

LEFT: Had this Italian fountain, composed of classical statuary and arcing jets, been placed in a less secluded spot, the appealing sense of intimacy would have been lost. To emulate this design, set a statuary fountain in a spot where it will be framed against an evocative background. If you can't manage a verdant grotto, a backdrop of rocks or even a fence can render a similar effect.

OPPOSITE: A trickle of water trails from a seashell into a little pool of stones; the concentration that the statue of the young woman brings to her task tends to mesmerize her audience as well. This unorthodox style of fountain is well-suited to a small garden or patio area, where the sculpture can be tucked into a pleasant spot, as if it is merely a regular visitor to the garden.

ABOVE: A sculpted basin is a classic choice for a formal landscape. In addition to the tinkling jet of water in the top, this fountain adds the surprise of spouting lions below. The artful show is achieved with concealed piping and under-water pump.

OPPOSITE: Owners of small gardens are often advised to "go up" by adding trellises or vines along walls and fences. But a wall fountain might be the most irresistible option—the necessary plumbing hardware and basin can easily be hidden from view. And the pool into which the water spills from the mounted face (or any other statuary of your choosing) need not be especially wide or long to accommodate its captivating stream of water.

ABOVE: Natural materials like this jumble of rocks and small boulders are ideal spillways. Careful placement will control the way the water flows and falls. The sound will be most animated if you can rig it so that water descends from varying heights and some of the flows are broad while others are narrow.

RIGHT: Sculpted birds perch sweetly at the edge of a diminutive fountain, providing graceful accent to a small garden. An interesting variation on the usual fountain form, water from the shallow basin cascades in a wide stripe to the pool below.

ABOVE: Fountains can also be small and subtle, like this earthenware bowl tucked in among lush greenery. Adding the mysterious, half-submerged sculpture of a face seems to hint at a strange tale, while the array of upturned faces ranged behind furthers the intrigue. Those who happen upon this enigmatic vignette will halt in their tracks to ponder the sight.

OPPOSITE: Long a staple of Japanese-style gardens, the eternally flowing bamboo spout appears in many forms— and can easily be varied to suit your space. The basin may be a large, narrow-necked jar as shown here, which generates a deep, bass sound, or you may opt for a broader, more open bowl, with its lighter, brighter music.

ABOVE: A small pedestal fountain is the centerpiece of an all-white planting. Note that the natural clay color of the fountain is in contrast to, but not incongruous with, the garden's cool green foliage. The fountain's ivy motif links the feature subtly but firmly to the surrounding space.

ABOVE: Spilling, splashing, spraying, and lapping, this animated fountain gains superb drama from a generous flow of water. All this is achieved with elements that are not visible to the astounded viewer—internal and underwater piping and a submerged pump. When planning something this dramatic, make sure to get a powerful pump that is equal to the job. The higher the water needs to go (the further it has to travel from the main pool), the stronger the pump must be.

ABOVE: Set within a tiny pool, this glazed ceramic urn in deep cobalt is both beautiful and eminently practicable. The small bubbler in the center of the urn offers the suggestion of a fountain without the furor of a strong jet—instead, water flows gently in concentric ripples outward and over the edge of the pot, into the surrounding pool.

FORMAL FOUNTAINS

When you decide to install a formal fountain, your garden gains both grandeur and serenity. This holds true no matter how large or small the garden is. Any pool can be laid out so that it is in scale with its surroundings, as can the fountain itself, whether a simple jet or fan form or a "plumbed" statue such as a pensive nymph or whimsical frog (these are available in various materials, including lead, ceramic, and cast stone). The key is to select a fountain of appropriate size and a pump of adequate strength, so that the leaping, arching, spilling, or cascading water never falls outside the pool's borders. Then, depending on the size and weight of the fountain you choose, you may also have to install it atop a solid, level platform that gives it stability.

Formal fountains range from elaborate cast-iron affairs to simpler cast stone pieces, but all have in common the impression of dignity and grace. These pieces lend the landscape a majestic touch, invoking sensations of awe with their tempered streams and stately presence.

A well-done formal fountain—one that marries the sight and sound of splashing water with a planned, geometric layout and/or statuary—is a captivating sight and a sure garden focal point. The viewer cannot resist drawing near and is permitted flights of fancy no matter how mannered the feature is. And that, truly, is the magical power of such fountains—they sing within their bounds.

OPPOSITE: Here's an interesting variation on the often-seen tiered fountain—water spouts from all sides and various levels, creating an enchanting musical dance on the surface in the main basin below. Tall, clipped standards establish a secret space, while the peaceful palette of green invites a sense of calm.

RIGHT: This lively, multi-streamed, and tiered spray is achieved using a special fountain nozzle aptly called a "flower head." The sight is magnificent, and the sound as the droplets fall on the water below is a vivacious patter.

ABOVE: Fanciful statuary with classic themes—such as this head of Poseidon, Greek god of the sea, and its attending fish—give a formal fountain an air of intrigue. The viewer becomes enthralled, imagining the stories the sculptures suggest, even as the symmetrically spilling streams captivate the other senses.

ABOVE: An unusual wrought-iron fountain—an outdoor aquarium of sorts—draws visitors to a sheltered corner of this shady garden. Although most fountains are made from stone or concrete, wrought iron is also strong and weatherproof and thus an intriguing alternative. The scale of this diminutive fountain makes it a good choice for small-space gardens or for areas where you don't want the water feature to dominate the landscape.

ABOVE: When a lush, tumbling cascade is housed in a more dignified setting, the effect is daring—even a bit rebellious. The result is a display that is exciting, bringing the garden a liberating sense of motion and spontaneity without sacrificing its conventional lines.

OPPOSITE: A lofty jet of water creates a dramatic sight, enticing visitors from a distance and inspiring awe as they approach. Set in a ring-shaped pool within a circular plaza, the shape of the fountain echoes its geometric setting. For varying heights and shapes of spray, different types of fountain nozzles are available.

ABOVE: These aptly named, evenly spaced "flower sprays" conjure up images of a neat flower bed bursting with bloom, or perhaps a stage full of synchronized ballet dancers. This idea works well in a smaller pool, too, provided its shape is geometric.

RIGHT: A strict aboveground pool of solid form and rectangular lines cries out for the lighthearted presence of a fountain. The relatively small circle of this fountain's spray leaves enough water surface to act as a reflecting pool. Make the fountain compatible with the formal scene by centering it in the middle, then enjoy its lively contribution.

ABOVE: In a garden founded on neat lines and well-tended plants, your best bet is to select a fountain with a simple profile. Anything more elaborate than this single thin jet would compromise the setting's soothing appeal and restful elegance.

OPPOSITE: It's a surprising place to find a fountain—practically overhead and spouting a generous stream from on high. The genius of this design is that the garden immediately seems both larger and more intriguing. Route the spray through an impressive piece of statuary, and you have a grand sight indeed.

LEFT: Fountains needn't always spray water aloft. Here, a conventional stone fountain brings all its benefits to the garden, but its modest downward-arching streams allow the surroundings to remain in focus for the viewer. Observe how the gentle arcs of the water echo the vaulted tunnel of golden-flowered laburnum trees overhead. Deliberate or coincidental, this juxtaposition certainly adds grace to the peaceful scene.

OPPOSITE: This detail from a fountain at the Villa Ile de France shows just how much a sculpture with a human figure can do for a formal water feature. The smiling gaze of the young woman brings a smile to our own lips, causing us to slow our steps and wonder what she is admiring. Her own reflection? The soothing water? Or the intriguing creature or structure upon which she rests? Just pondering the question is reason enough to enjoy the pause.

ABOVE: A key ingredient in small courtyard gardens is a centering fountain, which provides focus and elegant ornament. The tiered design adds height, as do the flanking trees—the result is a feeling of lavishness and expansiveness in limited space.

OPPOSITE: Influenced by the classic courtyard fountains of Moorish Spain, this diminutive example contains all the basic elements that make these pieces so enticing: beautiful, hand-painted tilework; bright colors; a kinetic geometric shape; and statuary that enhances rather than overwhelms the whole. By plumbing the sidelined creatures as well as the center fountain, the sense of perpetually supplied water adds narrative charm.

ABOVE: Known as a "flower spray" or "tiered" fountain, individual streams of water travel to varying heights, rendering a somewhat irregular spray. This popular form brings many benefits to a pool: you get to savor the tinkling music of falling water and to view the varied patterns of the droplets, all while the water below gains plenty of beneficial aeration.

ABOVE: Accompanied by a leaping fish, this "water goddess" statue presides over a small pool whose edges are lined with little individual jets that spray inward. The simple yet elegant white flowers that border the pool also compel the eye toward the middle. The result is a highly classical display that revels in its self-contained beauty.

SPLASHING SPRINGS

I f you love the sight and sound of water, there are many ways to enjoy it in your garden without installing a feature that is formal or fancy. Casual or natural-style fountains take their inspiration more directly from nature, both in their design and in the random or spontaneous way the water flows. You can delight in anything from a bubbling spring to a shimmering cascade. When you select the source from which the water emerges, enhance the sight by choosing something made of natural materials—handsome stonework, rustic bricks, or even earthenware. The possibilities are endless and exciting.

The prettiest of such fountains are flanked by complementary landscaping. Take your cue from the springs found in nature, and let plants grow freely so that they envelop or lean over the water. If foliage trails in the water or the occasional group of fallen leaves or spent flowers eddies in the pool, let it be. If plants are growing in the water, allow them to spread as they wish and bloom profusely. There is great appeal in such unsophisticated scenes. The moving water and the lush growth will share a spirited partnership, just as nature intended.

Remember, though, that all naturalistic fountains are a magical illusion, brought to life by the careful choice of materials and the appropriate pipes, pump, and, sometimes, leak-proof liners. Enlist the aid of a professional who has experience with such projects, consult with water-garden suppliers, and/or do a little homework on the technical aspects. Quality workmanship and savvy installation will result in a spot whose sight and myriad sounds you will treasure.

OPPOSITE: Falling leaves, falling water—this enchanting little tiered fountain conjures an unaffected, pleasant sense of harmony with nature. The coppery color of the metal offers a further visual link with crisp autumn leaves. Encroaching herbage, while neat, is sufficiently lush enough to envelop the pool. The effect is reminiscent of a small woodland spring.

RIGHT: Tiny garden? How about a tiny fountain? The principle of "going upward when you can't go outward" is a stunning success in this ingenious display; water spills merrily down through four levels on its way into the ceramic pot. The elegant clay saucers that act as sluices are beautifully in keeping with the earthy colors and verdant greenery of this patio.

LEFT: Shop around and you will be enchanted by the diversity of fountain forms designed by creative sculptors. Though oversized, this realistic-looking leaf basin fits easily into a secluded nook; its tiny bubbler imparts the welcome, subtle tinkle of moving water.

OPPOSITE: In many climates, a cascade can continue to run in winter, offering pleasure to those who venture out to admire it. In winter many garden accents, hardscape elements, and water features take on a fresh beauty as they ornament the stark landscape. The continuously running water also benefits any fish or plants that may be wintering over deep below by helping to keep the water aerated and free of ice.

OPPOSITE: Asian-style gardens seem to call for more symmetry and simplicity than many fountains can supply. These humble but beautifully crafted urns fit the bill perfectly as each receives a single ribbon of water from a bamboo pipe. One set would have been an entrancing sight; the presence of three makes an even stronger impression, particularly in synchronized sound.

RIGHT: The great gardens of the Vatican in Rome include this long but simply executed series of wall fountains. Two tiers of gently pouring water create double the impact. Note that the site is thoroughly shaded by mature trees. If your own garden has such a spot and you have struggled with growing plants there, perhaps a fountain offers the perfect solution.

ABOVE: A fascinating variety of materials, from handfuls of seashells and smooth stones to stacks of salvaged bricks to highly contrived symmetrical sculptures flanking the head of the pool conspire to make a unique show. Add the sliding rills of flowing water and you have a truly artful marriage of the natural and the manmade.

ABOVE: New life for pottery—this ingenious, amusing fountain simply upends a few surplus pots. The already-present drainage holes make it simple to install the necessary fountain plumbing. Another plus: the contraption is small and can easily be tucked into a corner, where its novel presence will be exclaimed over.

RIGHT: Gossamer sheets of water glide over an elevated rocky promontory in a garden corner. The sound is gentler than a full, roaring waterfall, making for a soothing display.

ABOVE: There is a wide range of delightful creatures you might be willing to invite into your water garden—as plumbed fountains. Many emit a spray from their mouth; if you happen upon one that doesn't, such as this backward-glancing snail with watery antennae, you'll have a real conversation piece.

ABOVE: It looks natural, but this enchanting manmade waterfall brings a spontaneous beauty to a secluded nook. The trick is to install both rocks and pool securely and use a lower-strength pump so that the water spills rather than spews over the lip at the top.

ABOVE: Stonework in every aspect of this setting—the fountain, the basin, and even the surrounding patio—creates a charmingly unpretentious display. Note the way that the small faucet and its simple stream eternally splashing below are in scale with each other, making for a fountain that murmurs rather than shouts.

ABOVE: Just as the most interesting gardens combine textures as well as colors, so do intriguing fountains. The aqua patina of the botanical sculpture is lovely against the soft, aged pink of the brickwork; both materials have an appealing rough-smooth surface that invites touching.

ABOVE: A bubbler of water froths out of a rock in this pool's center, a fountain that is truly in harmony with its rock-lined perimeter. The water slides softly down the rock as it returns to the pool, thus eliminating the heavy splashing that would otherwise disturb the waterlilies and other plants growing nearby.

INTEGRATING A FOUNTAIN INTO THE LANDSCAPE

No matter what sort of garden you have—large or small, sunny or shady, formal or naturalistic, busy with plants or serene in its simplicity—a fountain is an inspired addition. With careful placement, it can become a focal point that the rest of the yard flatters. Or you can tuck it into a hidden corner to create an element of mystery or surprise. Either way, the trick is to make the fountain a part of the landscape, so its charms are highlighted yet it looks like it belongs.

If you already have a garden in place and don't wish to make major adjustments to the placement of your plants, you'll need to choose a display that will be compatible in size and style to the existing garden. Perhaps all that is needed is to clear out a small area, digging up and moving only a handful of plants. Or perhaps you have a focal point of some kind that you are not happy with, such as a birdbath, sundial, or garden sculpture, and you plan to simply replace it with a water show.

OPPOSITE: Semishady gardens are naturals for fountains because the constant play of sun and shade matches the random leaping, dancing movement of the water. A jet that shoots up into the air is a wise choice because it will be most visible against the dark backdrop of nearby trees. Centered on a small peninsula that juts out from a woodland garden, this display is guaranteed to capture visitors' attention.

RIGHT: Where space is limited, small and simple designs are best. This aboveground catch basin fed by the small stream issuing from the sculpted face succeeds in bringing the sight and sound of water to a restricted space. The gardener has made the most out of this wall fountain by elevating it slightly on stones and surrounding it by a symmetrical complement of handsome plants and fencework.

It is admittedly easier to design around a fountain feature. In other words, if you can, the best approach is to select and install the fountain, then add in complementary elements such as a patio, stonework, and/or landscaping once the water feature is in place. To do this, you need a firm vision of the effect you want. Consider the size and style of your house and the expanse of the garden space, as well as your dreams for the type of fountain you'd like and, of course, the amount you can afford to spend on the total project. A plan on paper (whether a rough sketch or the contracted design of a professional landscaper) is wise. Of course, like any other garden addition, you may discover that this one has a life of its own, and inspirations for minor adjustments to the fountain or its surroundings will come easily.

ABOVE: The place where garden paths merge is a perfect setting for a water feature. Various sorts of fountains would work here, but a circular-shaped, gurgling millstone fountain filled with and flanked by smooth, round stones is an inspired choice because they further echo the shape of the clearing. The fountain's understated character helps to define the tone for this garden as a place of quiet beauty.

OPPOSITE: Larger gardens call for high drama. Here a slender but towering geyser creates a grand effect without disturbing the aquatic plants in other parts of the pool. It also works well with the garden's columnar evergreens and the weeping willows; a smaller spray would be lost in such a setting.

ABOVE: Though more modest in size than the grand fountains of European gardens, this one creates the same magnificent drama, thanks to its lushly landscaped edges and centered gushing spray. The trick is to not make the display too cluttered or complex; note that there are plenty of plants, but not a lot of different kinds.

OPPOSITE: Ebullient wildflowers and herbs are in good company with the lively tiered fountain in the background. Both seem to bounce in the breeze, and greet a sunny day with eagerness. While a lower, more natural-looking fountain might have seemed like the obvious choice in this meadow setting, the high, sparkling jets of water create a more dramatic impact.

ABOVE: Selecting a fountain that is in scale with its setting is key—remember to take into account the height of the water jets as well as the sculpture itself. This fountain, viewed from a few yards away, sprays only slightly higher than the adjacent perennials and low wall.

OPPOSITE: The elegant beauty of a single spray arching upward brings serenity and interest to a shady area. The pretty violas that ring the pool provide definition to its edges but don't steal the show. The shadows of the pool act in opposition to the shimmering light on the distant gazebo, providing a stunning contrast between these two garden elements.

ABOVE: A swimming pool with a fountain? Why not? The dancing figure and the single shooting spray both direct the eye into the inviting water surface, adding the right touch of activity to a relaxing scene.

ABOVE: This fountain at the mission in Carmel, California, provides a classic example of the Spanish style. A hexagonal basin is centered with a bowl-shaped fountain; the edges of the basin are low and wide enough to sit on, inviting visitors to pause and contemplate the pretty garden or the water's sprinkled surface, or to trail a hand in the cooling water. The earthy color of both basin and fountain echo the hues of adobe walls and tile roof, offering a simple lesson in matching garden features to architecture.

267

ABOVE: Because this garden has a serene mood, and even includes a chair set out to invite rest and contemplation, a subtler fountain is a wise choice. This foaming fountain head calmly enhances the garden rather than taking the spotlight. Note that, because of the fountain's supporting role in the garden, the pool has been sited against the wall of a greenhouse rather than in the center of the lawn.

ABOVE: A long, narrow fountain display is the perfect way to introduce water to an attenuated garden space. Installing several smaller jets along the waterway keeps the eye moving and works well with the symmetrical layout of the adjacent flower borders. If there's room, an additional, aboveground fountain at the end gives the garden a dramatic destination or focal point.

ABOVE: A truly inspired designer added this unusual shallow fountain to the formal terrace. The pool has a strictly defined domain, as do the terra-cotta pots that stand in attendance. But like the lush evergreens that fill those pots, the splashing rills of water offer a measured impression of vitality, even exuberance.

PLANTINGS TO ACCENT A FOUNTAIN

The most memorable fountains fit into a garden with ease because they have been flanked or surrounded by attractive, complementary landscaping. Even a small or modest-looking fountain can be greatly enhanced by well-chosen plantings; large fountains also require thoughtful plant choices. But the intent is always the same: to create an oasis, a place to pause and enjoy the sight and sound of water in the gentle company of flowers and greenery.

You may choose plants that echo or repeat the action of the water. Many plants seem to "fountain" up out of the earth, with their foliage turning outward and arching down at the tips. Notice also how many flowers surge upward. Even shrubs and trees can imitate or enhance the form of flowing water, leaning protectively over the surface. Any of these options—carefully chosen to be in scale with the fountain's form and sensitively sited—add greatly to the spot's beauty and drama.

Another approach is to plant as if you were framing a picture, which in a sense, you are. Plants of modest mounding habits are naturals for this job. Alternatively, use exclusively one plant or one color, or create a simple, repeatable pattern around the pool or basin's perimeter. Just remember that your goal is to direct attention to the water itself and especially to the activity of the flowing or spouting water.

One other way to go is to allow, or put in place, surrounding plants that make a backdrop for the play of water. Dark, dense foliage such as that of evergreens—hedges, shrubs, or trees—are ideal, as are broadleaf evergreens. Whatever plants you choose to accent your fountain, remember that the idea is to focus on the water show and let the landscaping play a supportive but secondary role.

ABOVE: Sculpture that is complex and especially striking should be enjoyed with minimal distractions, which is why this magnificent ram's head fountain is modestly flanked by nothing more than trailing ivy and green topiary. The result is a display that has an established yet intriguing air to it, as if you had stumbled upon an ancient, hidden garden.

OPPOSITE: This fan-style fountain already provides so much vertical interest that the array of low-growing, horizontally spreading plants at its feet are a welcome sight. Observe, though, how subtly but aptly the straplike foliage of a lone iris, just behind the fountain, mimics the spray's form.

ABOVE: When a garden is given over to more than one fountain, there are many landscaping opportunities. Here, the fountain composed of a stout collection of ascending basins is attended by a lush assortment of taller bloomers, giving it weight and majesty. Meanwhile, the slim, tall spray to the left is not encroached upon by the landscaping, so it can play freely out in the open.

ABOVE: Bright flowers gather at the base of this lovely, single-jet fountain, delighting the eye even as they direct attention to what is above and ahead. The dark foliage behind the fountain makes an ideal backdrop for the water stream.

ABOVE: This Japanese-style fountain combines the refined form of urn-shaped bowls with a traditional bamboo spout that gently and perpetually spills water. By placing the feature facing outward from the base of a slope, and by choosing plants with cascading habits, the direction of the flow of the water seems natural, indeed inevitable.

OPPOSITE: In a densely planted area, a tall, flashy fountain would not only look out of place, it would probably hinder the healthy growth of these lovers of still water. The solution? Install a foaming fountain head, which makes splendid musical sounds but keeps splashing within a discrete area. A base of stones around the water further limits disturbances.

RIGHT: Simplicity rules in this shady nook, where a single ribbon of water is delivered to a small trough. Brightness is injected not only by the merry sound but by a bit of variegated foliage (the hosta, the iris spears) and a white calla lily.

OPPOSITE TOP: Water is cooling. So is shade. The perfect marriage occurs in a modest formal fountain under a canopy of established trees. The small basin is rimmed only by a monochromatic color scheme provided by shade-loving, profuse-blooming tuberous begonias.

OPPOSITE BOTTOM: In a big pool occupied by a variety of aquatic plants, this rushing, spilling spray occupies a central spot. Here its flow does not disturb the motion-sensitive lilypads. Notice also how the clump-forming blooming flowers such as canna occupy about the same amount of surface space as the fountain and its stone—this way they don't crowd it or unduly divert our attention.

ABOVE: Why not create a grotto in your garden, with all the secret, splashing lushness that the feature implies? Here, a small pool has been tucked into a corner and surrounded by generous foliage plants, especially lush clumps of ferns, which adore such damp, shady conditions.

OPPOSITE: Carefully chosen statuary, such as an attentive nymph, and a handful of lush "fountain-form" plants help make a water feature its own charming little world. Ornamental grasses, like these green and gold specimens, are favorite pairings for fountains. With the right balance of materials and plants, you can create a magical haven to which you can retreat and let your imagination wander.

ABOVE: Unusual fountains call for dramatic landscaping that complements but doesn't usurp the scene. The above-ground pool and surrounding brick walk give this elaborate fountain all the room it needs; exciting, bright flowers beyond that boundary, such as long-blooming rudbeckias, help set the lively tone.

ABOVE: Here, well-chosen flowers enhance the diminutive fountain display—the lilies, especially, echo the spray's profile. A plus: lilies are generally long bloomers, so the display can be enjoyed for weeks on end.

SOURCES

Anderson Design
P.O. Box 4057 C
Bellingham, WA 98227
800-947-7697
*Arbors, trellises, gates, and pyramids
(Oriental, modern, and traditional style)*

Barlow Tyrie Inc.
1263 Glen Avenue Suite 230
Moorestown, NJ 08057-1139
609-273-7878
*Teak wood garden furniture in English
garden style*

Boston Turning Works
42 Plymouth Street
Boston, MA 02118
617-482-9085
$1 for brochure
*Distinctive wood finials for gates,
fenceposts, and balustrades*

Brooks Barrel Company
P.O. Box 1056
Department GD25
Cambridge, MD 21613-1046
410-228-0790
$2 for brochure
*Natural-finish pine wooden barrels and
planters*

Charleston Gardens
61 Queen Street
Charleston, SC 29401
803-723-0252
$3 catalog
Fine garden furnishings

Doner Design Inc.
Department G
2175 Beaver Valley Pike
New Providence, PA 17560
717-786-8891
Free brochure
Handcrafted landscape lights (copper)

Florentine Craftsmen Inc.
46-24 28th Street
Department GD
Long Island City, NY 11101
718-937-7632
*Garden furniture, ornaments, fountains,
and statuary of lead, stone, and bronze*

Flower Framers by Jay
671 Wilmer Avenue
Cincinnati, Ohio 45226
Flower boxes

FrenchWyres
P.O. Box 131655
Tyler, TX 75713
903-597-8322
$4 catalog
*Wire garden furnishings: trellis, urns,
cachepots, window boxes, arches, and
plant stands*

Gardenia
9 Remington Street
Cambridge, MA 02138
800-685-8866
Birdhouses

Gardensheds
651 Millcross Road
Lancaster, PA 17601
$4 for brochure
*Potting sheds, wood boxes, and larger
storage units*

Hooks Lattice
7949 Silverton Avenue #903
San Diego, CA 92126
800-896-0978
Free catalog
Handcrafted wrought-iron gardenware

Kenneth Lynch & Sons
84 Danbury Road
P.O. Box 488
WIlton, CT 06897
203-762-8363
Free brochure
*Benches, gates, sculpture and statuary,
planters and urns, topiary, sundials,
and weathervanes*

Kinsman Company
River Road
Department 351
Point Pleasant, PA 18950
800-733-4146
Free catalog
*European plant supports, pillars, arches
trellises, flowerpots, and planters*

Lake Creek Garden Features Inc.
P.O. Box 118
Lake City, IA 51449
712-464-8924
Free brochure
*Obelisks, plant stands, and gazing globes
and stands*

Liteform Designs
P.O. Box 3316
Portland, OR 97208
503-253-1210
*Garden lighting: path, bullard, accent,
step, and tree fixtures*

New Blue Moon Studio
P.O. Box 579
Leavenworth, WA 98826
509-548-4754
*Trellises, gates, arbors, and garden
furniture*

New England Garden Ornaments
P.O. Box 235
38 East Brookfield Road
North Brookfield, MA 01535
508-867-4474
Free brochure, $8 for catalog
package
*Garden fountains and statuary, planters
and urns, antique furniture, sundials, and
limestone ornaments*

Northwoods Nursery
27368 South Oglesby
Canby, OR 97013
503-266-5432
Free catalog and growing guide
*Nursery features, ornamental trees, shrubs,
and vines*

Secret Garden
c/o Christine Sibley
15 Waddell Street N.E.
Atlanta, GA 30307
Garden sculpture

Stone Forest
Department G
P.O. Box 2840
Sante Fe, NM 87504
505-986-8883
*Hand-carved granite birdbaths, basins,
fountains, lanterns, and spheres*

Sycamore Creek
P.O. Box 16
Ancram, NY 12502
Handcrafted copper garden furnishings

Tanglewood Conservatories
Silver Spring, MD
Free brochure
*Handcrafted period glass houses and
atriums*

Tidewater Workshop
Oceanville, NJ 08231
800-666-8433
Free catalog
*White cedar benches, chairs, swings,
and tables*

Toscano
17 East Campbell Street
Department G881
Arlington Heights, IL 60005
800-525-1733
Free catalog
*Historic garden sculptures, including
seraphs and cherubs, and French tapestries*

Valcovic Cornell Design
Box 380
Beverly, MA 01915
$4 for catalog, redeemable with
purchase
*Trellises and arbor benches (traditional to
contemporary style)*

Van Engelen Inc.
23 Tulip Drive
Bantam, CT 06750
860-567-8734
Free catalog
*Exotic bulbs and hybrid flowers (crocus,
lilies, tulips, daffodils)*

Van Ness Water Gardens
2460 North Euclid
Deptartment 942
Upland, CA 91784-1199
800-205-2425
*Water lilies, bog plants, and a variety of
plants for water gardens*

Vixen Hill Manufacturing
Company
Main Street
Elverson, PA 19520
800-423-2766
Cedar gazebos and screened garden houses

Wayside Gardens
1 Garden Lane
Hodges, SC 29695-0001
Free catalog
*Worldwide ornamental garden plants and
hardy bulbs*

Weatherend Estate Furniture
6 Gordon Drive
Rockland, ME 04841
800-456-6483
Heirloom-quality garden furniture

Wood Classics
Box 96G0410
Gardiner, NY 12525
914-255-5651
Free catalog
*Garden benches, swings, chairs and tables,
rockers, lounges, and umbrellas (all teak
and mahogany outdoor furniture)*

CANADIAN SOURCES

Corn Hill Nursery Ltd.
RR 5
Petitcodiac NB EOA 2HO

Ferncliff Gardens
SS 1
Mission, British Columbia
V2V 5V6

McFayden Seed Co. Ltd.
Box 1800
Brandon, Manitoba
R7A 6N4

Stirling Perennials
RR 1
Morpeth, Ontario
N0P 1X0

PHOTO CREDITS

A-Z Botanical Collection: 95, 118, 132 bottom, 175, 185, 276

©Rick Darke: 244

©R. Todd Davis: 85 left, 100 left, 120, 136, 200, 255, 275

©Derek Fell: 220, 226, 227, 233, 236–237, 241, 243, 249, 250, 251, 254, 262, 264, 266, 267, 276 top, 279

The Garden Picture Library: 2; ©Mark Bolton: 170 left; ©Lynne Brotchie: 86 left, 116, 117, 181, 210; ©Linda Burgess: 162, 231; ©Brian Carter: 177; ©Eric Crichton: 176; ©Henk Dijkman: 48 right; ©Ron Evans: 54, 199; ©Christopher Fairweather: 10–11, 46; ©John Glover: 32–33, 110, 115, 171, 194, 216; ©Sunniva Harte: 67; ©Marike Heuff: 159, 169; ©Neil Holmes: 14, 273; ©Jacqui Hurst: 157; ©Lamontagne: 160, 163, 189, 201, 272; ©Marianne Majerus: 178; ©Mayer/Lescanff: 153; ©Zara McCalmont: 187; ©Marie O'Hara: 65; ©Gary Rogers: 212 left; ©David Russel: 149; ©J.S. Sira: 38, 232, 274; ©Janet Sorrell: 192, 265; ©Friedrich Strauss: 80, 91 top and bottom, 104, 105, 139 both, 142–143, 144 both; ©Ron Sutherland: 158, 165, 170 right, 188, 207 right; ©Brigette Thomas: 13, 34, 42, 148, 164, 184, 190; ©Juliette Wade: 36 right; ©Steven Wooster: 46, 94, 128 left, 134, 208, 228 right

©Anne Gordon: 222

Houses and Interiors: 81, 88, 150 right, 182, 183, 197, 198

©Andrea Jones: 240, 263, 268 left

©Dency Kane: 15, 101, 132, 211 right, 212–213, 218, 223, 245

©Lynn Karlin: 25, 48 left, 51, 52, 55, 63, 74 right

©Marianne Majerus: 89, 109, 112, 114, 128–129, 130, 131, 141, 166 left, 176, 186, 192 right, 202, 204, 206–207, 211 left

©Allan Mandell: 63

©Charles Mann: 18 left, 19, 20, 21, 22, 23, 27, 30, 44, 56 left, 57, 58, 61, 62, 64 left, 70 right, 72, 75, 82, 83, 90, 92, 93, 98, 103, 123, 126, 136 (Designer: Keeyla Meadows), 137, 140 (Designer: Bob Clark), 145, 150 left, 154, 161, 172, 173

©Clive Nichols: 6, 7, 8, 9, 31 both, 35, 36 left, 37 (Designer: Olivia Clarke), 40 left (Designer: Paula Rainey Crofts), 49 (Designer: Julie Toll), 53 (Designer: Anthony Noel), 59 (Designer: Claus Scheinert), 64 right (Designer: Jonathan Bailie), 66, 68 (Designer: Elizabeth Woodhouse), 69 left, 73 (Designer: Elizabeth Woodhouse), 76 both, 77, 78–79, 107 (Designer: Joan Murdy), 108, 111 (Designer: Anthony Noel), 122 right (Designer: Emma Lush), 125 (Designer: Fiona Lawrenson), 135 (Designer: Emma Lush) 146–147, 168 169 left, 174, 179, 193, 196, 214

©Hugh Palmer: 219, 230, 234, 235, 238, 239, 242, 246, 256 right, 258, 261, 270

H. Armstrong Roberts: ©F. Sieb: 280

©Nancy S. Trueworthy: 86–87, 113, 133, 138, 155, 166–167, 203, 257, 278